MW00910469

# Pocket
# Menu Reader
## China

Emanuela Rossi

LANGENSCHEIDT

NEW YORK · BERLIN · MUNICH · VIENNA · ZURICH

Originally published in Italy under the title:

DIZIONARIO DEL MENU – CINA
L'Airone Editrice
2001 © E. G. E. s. r. l. – Rome

English translation:
Angie McNee

Cover photo:
Stock Food, Munich

© 2001 by Langenscheidt Publishers, Inc.
Maspeth, N.Y. 11378
Printed in Germany

# NOTE ON PRONUNCIATION

For over two thousand years, written Chinese has been the common denominator in an immense country inhabited by different peoples, each with their own customs and dialects. It is based on several thousands of ideograms (approximately 60,000, with a history that, in some cases, goes back 5,000 years), which are pronounced very differently from one region to another. To resolve the inevitable problems created by this situation, with the foundation of the People's Republic of China an official language was adopted – the so-called Mandarin Chinese – which roughly corresponds to the spoken dialect in the Beijing area. For the same reason, a single system of phonetic transcription, called *Pinyin*, was introduced, based on Russian and German pronunciation, which has now replaced all precedents.

Since the rules of this system of transcription are rather complicated, in this handbook the pronunciation in Pinyin is accompanied by the transliteration of the Chinese characters, so that users who do not speak Chinese can easily read the words and consequently make themselves understood. So, in italics next to the transcription in Pinyin of the Chinese terms you will find the pronunciation in "English", or rather in the form that is easiest to read and at the same time closest to the Chinese pronunciation.

# *INTRODUCTION*

It would have been impossible for a civilization boasting 5,000 years of history to neglect an art as important as gastronomy. And in fact Chinese cuisine stands out for its incredible diversity, which derives from the meeting of very different cultures, natural environments and climates, as well as for its exquisite delicacy, reflecting the taste for the pleasures of life that has always characterized the courts of the emperors and Mandarins. Today, as in days gone by, the culinary art must satisfy the senses of sight and smell as well as being tasty and healthy. This is why a Chinese meal combines the five tastes (salty, sweet, bitter, spicy and sour), the five consistencies (soft, crisp, liquid, dry and gelatinous) and the three temperatures (hot, cold and scalding). The dishes alternate between cold and hot, salty and sweet, crisp and gelatinous, according to the rules of harmony of flavors, colors and form, to create the perfect balance that is so pleasing to the spirit and to the senses.

The Chinese philosopher Confucius said that a good meal is eaten first with the eyes, then with the nose and finally with the mouth. Chinese cuisine combines science (the methods of cooking), philosophy (the variety of ingredients) and art (the presentation). Cooking is an art that stimulates the intellect and the imagination – you need look no further than the names of the dishes – and eating becomes an act of balance and beauty.

Those of you who are lucky enough to go to China will have the pleasure of tasting the dishes described in this small guide and of trying all the others which, due to the lack of space and the inexhaustible nature of the subject matter, have not been included. Moreover, if you are brave enough to put excessive concerns with hygiene to one side, you will also be able to taste the kebabs, the pizza-like breads, the soups and the sweets prepared on the bustling streets of Canton or in villages of the remote Sichuan countryside: they will have the precious flavor of full immersion in the real China. Not only the *haute cuisine* but also the modest offerings prepared at humble restaurants or knocked together in the street – which are no less tasty or varied for their modesty – merit being studied and enjoyed.

And so, three times a day we can draw near to a culture that is otherwise a million miles from our own, by way of the most basic of things: food. You will discover similarities and differences and, with a few short phrases to hand, you will astound the Chinese who, overcoming their natural reserve, will not fail to praise you for your efforts to communicate. Eating and fellowship are activities that can bring us closer to people of a different culture, enriching us and making us more open-minded and tolerant. So let's raise our glass in that most symbolic of gestures: *cheers*. This age-old form of greeting and courtesy originated in China…

## WHAT THE CHINESE EAT

To begin our gastronomic tour of China with breakfast is to risk conforming to the stereotype of the American who eats nothing but hamburgers and fries; it will also potentially lead to disillusionment. The concept of breakfast in China is completely different to what it is in the West – so much so that even the English, who are used to knocking back eggs and bacon at seven o' clock in the morning, struggle to eat cucumbers and onions in soy sauce, spicy condiments, gelatinous soups and heavy deep-fried food, all washed down with several glasses of beer. Furthermore, our first experience of Chinese food is made more difficult still by the absence of our own breakfast staples of bread, milk and coffee.

It must be remembered that in China there is no link between what is eaten and when: the single aim is to combine a good variety of nutritious foods. Chinese cuisine is based on two distinct elements: "fan" (*fan*), the basic dish, comprising of a cereal (usually rice, but also wheat, barley, millet, maize, etc.), and "cai" (*tsai*), or rather everything that goes with the basic dish (meat, fish, vegetables, tofu and various sauces). The daily meal, which is quick and light, is always made up of these two components, thereby ensuring a balanced intake of the different nutrients: a bowl of rice is eaten together with a little meat, a little fish and some vegetables.

It can seem to the first-time visitor to China that the population does nothing but eat. In some sense this is true; the Chinese eat everything and at all times of the day and night. However, it is also true that meal times are early in relation to our own: lunch is at 11.30 and dinner at around 18.00. In the shops and in public offices it is not uncommon to see employees eating their food at the counter, holding their bowl close and carrying its contents to their mouth with a skilful flick of their chopsticks.

The most common meat in China is pork; in fact, on menus the word "rou" (*ro*, meat) always refers to it. Not a single part of the pig goes to waste – the Chinese even eat the trotters and the tail – and the entrails are considered a delicacy. The Chinese eat duck on special occasions and it can be slow and laborious to prepare. Fish (yu, *yoo*) is thought to bring good luck: the word for fish has the same pronunciation as the word for "plenty"; and for this reason it is eaten at Chinese New Year. Carp is the most sought-after fish, symbolizing courage because it swims against the current. Chinese sweets rarely agree with the western palate (they are anything but sweet, often rubbery and unappealing to the eye) but they are nevertheless worth tasting, if only for the experience.

## WHERE TO EAT

In China the choice of food is only succeeded by the choice of souvenirs: in both cases the visitor is spoilt for choice. You can eat for very little in the small eateries with outside tables (fanpu, *fan-poo*; fanguan, *fan-gwan*; xiaochidian, *siao-chr-dien*); alternatively there are medium-priced eating-places (jiulou, *jioh-lo*; jiudian, *jioh-dien*) or elegant restaurants (fandian, *fan-dien*; fanzhuang, *fan-jwang*). These are often to be found in the large hotels and are usually frequented by communist party officials and businessmen. Here there is almost always a menu in English and the quality of the food is generally high (but it is always wise to steer clear of the international cuisine). Many cities boast bustling and highly popular restaurants in what were once ancient inns: such is the case of the tavern belonging to Mrs. Chen of Chengdu, where you can try the famous *tofu of the pock-marked old lady* (mapo doufu, see **National dishes**, p. 54), which is made according to a recipe that dates back 400 years, or of Goubuli in Tianjin, an informal eating-place established a century ago that serves delicate, melt-in-the-mouth *dim sum*. The name of this restaurant means "dog scatterer"; apparently this was the nickname of its founder, a man so ugly that not even dogs had the courage to look at him. Goubuli is also the name of the house specialty, a kind of bread filled with spicy, succulent pork.

## THE CHINESE TABLE

In China, the table is always round. This is for two reasons: firstly, because the Chinese are great talkers and the circular shape is conducive to conversation; and secondly, in order to accommodate the rotating serving platform (zhuanpan, *jwan-pan*) on which the various dishes are set. In the limited space left by this cleverly designed table, you will find a small plate, a bowl and a ceramic soup spoon, a glass and, of course, the chopsticks (kuaizi, *kwai-ds*), which rest on elegant chopstick-holders of the most unusual shapes, which are set for each person. Contrary to practices in Chinese restaurants over here, where clients are often given the chopsticks as a present (and where, in any case, there is no objection to taking them away as a souvenir), in China the appropriation of these precious utensils (made from plastic or lacquered wood) is frowned upon and can anger the restaurant owner, since they are washed and reused like normal cutlery.

Things are different if we head for the "fanpu" (*fan-poo*), where the service is less ceremonious and the chopsticks are of the throw-away kind, made from bamboo: to ensure that they haven't been used by anyone else, check that they are joined at the end. In these eating-houses it is wise also to check (and perhaps wipe) the bowls and glasses, and to watch out for the tablecloth (when there is one), since the Chinese have a habit of wiping their mouths on the edge, leaving evidence of their meal. In the face of these minor discomforts, you can enjoy an atmosphere that is without doubt more real and more friendly than in the large, anonymous restaurants, and take away all the chopsticks that you want.

## THE BANQUET

Banquets are held on important occasions. This is the time to try special dishes, to make repeated toasts and, in particular, to order excessive amounts of food. In fact, to eat everything is considered impolite, the implication being that the host has been stingy in his provision; for the same reason rice rarely features among the courses (it is a humble food) and to ask for it amounts to saying that, despite the abundance of dishes, you have still not managed to eat your fill.

The banquet opens with a toast, which is repeated several times; the participants all raise their glass with both hands without letting it touch the others and shout "ganbei!" (gan-bay), which means literally *dry the glass!*

The meal begins with cold appetizers (jiucai, *jioh-tsai*) – these generally include various pickles and cold meats, hard-boiled eggs, peanuts – which are artistically presented and imaginatively decorated. The meal continues with numerous meat, fish, tofu and vegetable-based dishes (usually between 8 and 12, but a gala meal can consist of over 20).

There are no first courses, second courses and vegetable courses; rather, the dishes arrive in quick succession according to criteria that to us can seem illogical, but which respect the strict rules of taste and harmony between the flavors, aromas, consistency and presentation of the food: it is necessary to alternate *yang* foods and *yin* foods (see **Cuisine and medicine**, p. 35), i.e. foods that grow in the ground, which are dense, solid and strong, and foods that grow upwards, which are delicate, ethereal and fragmented. After the main dishes comes the soup, which aids digestion (it is never eaten at the start of the meal since this would make the host look like a miser who wanted to fill his guests immediately). The meal usually ends with a splendid freshwater fish, the symbol of abundance and luxury; cooked and served whole, complete with head and tail, it expresses the desire "to begin well and to end well". Only rarely are sweets and fruit brought out; the Chinese eat the latter between meals (but when it does appear it is always peeled, cut and elegantly presented).

In short, participation in a Chinese banquet is the climax

of this gastronomic experience; however, it also helps us to understand certain aspects of the culture of a faraway people, for example their strong sense of community: the banquet gives us a chance to share the pleasures of the table and of life in general, and to invite others to take part in our pleasure. Orders are not placed individually; the dishes on the rotating platform at the center of the table are meant to be shared among all the participants in the meal: each person helps himself or herself in turn, taking a bit from each of the various dishes, and in this way participating in the general enjoyment.

Water is not drinkable anywhere in China; it is always boiled (kai shui, *kai shweh*, which means literally "open water") and used to make tea, or left to cool (bingshui, *bing-shweh*). Bottled water is readily available but it does not taste very good and often it is not mineral water: it is simply *bingshui* or rather unpleasant-tasting distilled water. Imported mineral water (usually French) can be purchased at supermarkets, but it is expensive.

Roadside kiosks sell a wide variety of sugary drinks made from fruit – lychee, mango, coconut, banana, pear, pineapple – which are all very good and cheap. The Jianlibao fruit juices are the best.

Fresh milk is hard to find and very expensive, while the long-life variety is sold in large supermarkets. Yogurt is on sale all over the place, and is good and inexpensive. It comes in small glass bottles and is drunk through a straw. Inner Mongolia is home to "koumiss" (*komis*), a salty drink made from fermented horse's milk.

Coffee is available exclusively in large hotels and it is definitely to be avoided, both for its taste and for its price. During meals the Chinese drink beer, orangeade or Coca-Cola. They rarely drink wine and never tea (contrary to popular thought). Liqueurs and rice wine are brought out on special occasions and are sometimes drunk warm.

## Tea

Tea (cha, *cha*) is the most common beverage in the world; this is not hard to believe if you think that it is the national beverage of China, where over a billion people drink it every day. But in China, tea-drinking is an age-old custom that is thought to have curative properties. There are numerous legends concerning the origins of tea; these tend to play up the virtues of the plant and date it to the beginning of time. However, we know for a fact that it was customarily drunk in China in ancient times and that the plant (*Camelia sinesis*, an evergreen shrub of the Teacee family) was grown before the Christian era and used for medicinal purposes. It is interesting to note that in many western languages the word "tea" derives from the Chinese *cha*, such as *cha'i* in Russian, *çay* in Turkish, *shy* in Arabic; alternatively, by way of the Malay *t'e*, we get to the English *tea*, the German *tee* and the Italian *tè*.

The virtues of this plant have indeed been magnified to excess, but tea, and especially the green variety, does have some noteworthy qualities: it contains a small amount of caffeine, which speeds up the metabolism, and a high percentage of tannic acid, known for its anti-inflammatory and germicidal properties. Moreover, it can reduce and maintain cholesterol levels, stimulate digestion and reduce the assimilation of fats. For this reason it is of vital importance to people who live off sheep-farming and eat large quantities of meat, such as some ethnic minorities in China. Recent studies have revealed a link between this beverage and a reduction in the risk of developing cancer.

Today, despite the big invasion of Coca-Cola and other sweet beverages, tea continues to be the number one drink in China; wherever they go, the Chinese never fail to take their daily dose of this precious infusion. Tea is taken without sugar, milk or lemon, at all times and in all places; on the bus, in the shops, at the post office or strolling in the park, many people will be clutching a container filled with tea; the leaves are not filtered and so when the contents are finished more boiling water is simply poured over the top.

It is said that tea has cooling properties and that it can cure rheumatism; in southern China, where it is very humid, tea houses continue to thrive: people go there to chat, to play *mahjong* and – naturally – to knock back large quantities of tea. This is of a special kind, made from leaves that are practically unbroken; it is dried in a small amount of oil together with ginger and salt, then water is added and the preparation is set to boil. It is not worth trying, both because the suffocating heat in these places begs an ice-cold Coca-Cola rather than a hot tea, and because the taste of this infusion is not exactly congenial to our western palate. Contrarily, the mint infusion served in Yunnan is very pleasant, with or without tea.

Tea is cultivated in many parts of China and, since its characteristics vary according to climate and altitude, there are many varieties; the following is a general division based on the production process.

**Green tea** (lucha, *loo-cha*) 绿茶 This is the most common kind of tea and is produced mainly along the middle and lower sections of the Yangtze River. The leaves are harvested when still small and they are dried, usually left whole, without fermentation. This process gives the tea a subtle, delicate flavor and a color that ranges from jade green to bright yellow; in addition, the theine content is very low. Longjin (*dragon's well*), once reserved exclusively for the emperor, is the most superior kind, and is produced on the shores of the Western Lake near Hangzhou. Today, this tea is still mostly produced by hand, and only the most delicate shoots are picked; harvesting takes place between the end of March and the end of October at intervals of seven to ten days: if the leaves are allowed to grow beyond a certain point the quality of the tea declines. Four kilograms of leaves are required to produce one kilogram of Longjin tea.

Other select types include Maofeng, grown in the Yellow Mountains in Anhui, and Biluochun (*spring of the green snail*), which comes from Jiangsu.

**Black tea** (hongcha, *hong-cha*) 红茶 This is known as *red tea* in Chinese. The leaves are first ground or rolled, and then fermented and dried; this process gives rise to a pleasant amber color and a pungent taste that is stronger than green tea. The most popular kinds are Qihong, produced in Qimen in Anhui, Dianhong from Yunnan, Suhong from Jiangsu, Chuanhong from Sichuan and Huhong from Hunan.

# BEVERAGES

**Oolong tea** (wulongcha, *woo-long-cha*) 乌龙茶 *Tea of the black dragon* is a cross between green tea and black tea insofar as fermentation is interrupted when the heating process is only half complete; in this way the leaves become dark on the outside and remain green inside. The color of this tea ranges from golden brown to red-orange; it has a full and slightly fruity aroma that leaves a pleasant aftertaste. It is a specialty of the southeastern regions, especially Fujian, Guangdong and the island of Taiwan. The most famous sorts are Guanyin (*merciful Buddha*), Dong Ding (*frozen peaks*), Baihao (*white hair*) and Tie Guanyin (*iron Buddha*).

**Aromatic tea** (huacha, *hwa-cha*) 花茶 This is tea – usually of the green variety – to which flower petals, fruit, seeds or spices are added. The most common kinds are osmanthus (guihua, *gweh-hwa*), a scented fern, chrysanthemum (juhua, *joo-hwa*), magnolia (mulan, *moo-lan*) and jasmine (molihua, *moh-lee-hwa*), which has a distinctive and delicate perfume and is particularly common in northern China.

**Brick tea** (zhuancha, *jwan-cha*) 砖茶 This tea, made from coarsely ground twigs and leaves, is steamed and compressed into what are generally rectangular-shaped blocks. In this way it can be stored for a long time and is easy to transport. Produced in Sichuan and Yunnan, brick tea is also common in Tibet. Here it is left to infuse slowly, until black, after which salt and yak's butter are added; finally it is combined with a few handfuls (literally) of "zanba" (*dsam-pa*), a kind of polenta made from roasted barley flour, which is the Tibetans' staple food. The mixture is kneaded (again by hand) to obtain a fairly stiff dough, and this is washed down with additional large quantities of tea.

## Making tea according to the rules

To make tea the Chinese way, the following are important: the type of water, its temperature, the quantity of leaves, the length of infusion and the kind of teapot. In particular, the shape and color of the teapot must be in harmony with the cup and with the chosen variety of tea: in Chinese markets there are beautiful ceramic cups in white or blue, with drawings of dragons and landscapes, which come with a lid.

**Water**: it is best to use soft water with a low mineral content.
**Temperature**: this varies according to the quality and type of tea. To prepare fermented varieties the temperature must reach boiling point, while for green teas around 90 degrees is sufficient.
**Quantity**: this also varies according to the kind of tea. Green tea leaves are usually in one piece, while black tea leaves are broken up or finely ground, so a smaller quantity is required. Between a quarter and two-thirds of the teapot must be filled with leaves.
**Length of infusion**: the leaves are covered with water and

allowed to infuse for at least a minute. However, longer is required if the leaves have already been used.

**Teapot**: the best teapots are made from a special kind of clay called "zisha" (*ds-sha*), which reputedly keeps the tea perfectly even when left for weeks. Small and graceful, these teapots come with small cups without handles.


## Dishes with tea

Tea is used to make some delicious dishes.

**Duck with tea**. Duck steamed together with rice wine, ginger, aniseed and cinnamon, then flavored with roasted tea leaves and tea infusion.

**Pears in tea**. Pears cooked in black tea, sprinkled with sugar and served with orange juice. They make a light dessert.

**Shoulder of lamb with tea**. Shoulder of lamb fried lightly in peanut oil and then baked in an infusion of black tea, together with fresh black figs and thin slices of ginger.

**Marbled eggs**. The eggs are hard-boiled and their shells are tapped lightly until the surface of each is entirely covered in tiny cracks; following this, they are re-boiled, this time in an infusion of tea, together with aniseed, cinnamon and soy sauce. When the shells are removed, the eggs display beautiful marble-like veins and have a delicate taste.

## Wine and liqueurs

In the second millennium BC, the Chinese were already making alcoholic beverages by fermenting cereals such as millet, rice and sorghum. These liqueurs were still common even after the Arabs had introduced viticulture to China in the second century BC. In fact in Chinese the same word (jiu, *jioh*) is used to denote wine, liqueurs and all alcoholic drinks in general.

Wine and liqueurs have always been important to the Chinese: in the past, they customarily made drink-offerings as a sign of respect for their ancestors and to celebrate special feast days. Numerous poets and men of letters have drawn inspiration from alcohol-induced drunkenness: mandarins posted far from home and officials nearing the end of their career have faced the pain of loneliness and the separation from loved ones by turning to wine, finding in it comfort for their sorrows. The following lines by Li Po (701-762), one of the greatest poets of the Tang era, testify to this fact:

> *Among the flowers, a decanter of wine.*
> *I drink alone, without friends;*
> *but I raise my glass and beckon the pale moon:*
> *now the shadow in front of me makes us three.*
> *Moon you do not know the wine's drunkenness,*

> shadow you know only how to follow my body,
> companions of a moment, shadow and moon,
> we must celebrate while it is spring.
> I sing and the moon wavers up and down,
> I dance and my shadow follows me confusedly.
> Joy unites us while we are awake,
> then, inebriated, we separate;
> but united in eternity, unloved pilgrims,
> far away, among the clouds,
> we will meet again.

## LIQUEURS

Chinese liqueurs are made from the distillation of different cereals and can have a high alcohol content (over 50 percent proof); some are difficult to produce and are left to age slowly in ceramic vases buried underground. They are consumed at banquets and are sometimes drunk warm.

**Fenjiu** (*fen-jioh*) 汾酒 Typical of the city of Fenyang, this liqueur is mature and very strong (50 percent proof). It has a sweet, fresh aroma that leaves a pleasant aftertaste. The cereals are fermented in half-buried ceramic vases; after distillation they are allowed to ferment still further and distilled a second time. Liqueurs made in this way are aged separately.

**Gaoliangjiu** (*gao-liang-jioh*) 高粱酒 This is one of the most common liqueurs, made from distilled sorghum.

**Guandijiu** (*gwan-dee-jioh*) 馆帝酒 Produced in Sichuan, this liqueur is made from sorghum and wheat. It can be up to 54% proof.

**Gujinggong jiu** (*goo-jing-goong jioh*) 古井贡酒 This liqueur is typical of Anhui and is made from a distillate of wheat, barley, sorghum and black soya. Highly aromatic, sweet and refreshing, it is fairly high in alcohol (38 percent proof).

**Huangheluo jiu** (*hwang-heh-lwo jioh*) 黄鹤楼酒 Produced in the city of Wuhan, this liqueur is quite aromatic, sweet and refreshing.

**Jiannanchun jiu** (*jien-nan-choon jioh*) 剑南春酒 Aromatic, refreshing and highly alcoholic, this liqueur is made in Sichuan from distilled sorghum, corn, wheat, rice and glutinous rice.

**Jingjiu** (*jing-jioh*) 京酒 This product is obtained by distilling sorghum, wheat and glutinous rice. It can be up to 35% proof.

**Laojiuhan** (*lao-jioh-han*) 老酒汗 Typical of Zhejiang, this liqueur is made by distilling rice and red rice. Its alcohol content can approach 50 percent proof.

**Luzhou laojiao** (*loo-jo lao-jiao*) 泸州老窖 This is one of the most typical Chinese liqueurs. It is produced in Sichuan from a combination of sorghum, wheat, barley and rice.

# BEVERAGES

**Maotaijiu** (*mao-tai-jioh*) 茅台酒 Typical of the Guizhou region, this liqueur is made from sorghum. It has a delicate flavor that the Chinese liken to soy sauce.

**Meiguilu** (*may-gweh-loo*) 玫瑰露 This is the famous rose grappa, a liqueur that is flavored with rose petals; it is much more common abroad than in China itself, where it is drunk especially in the southern regions.

**Qingkejiu** (*ching-ke-jioh*) 青稞酒 Barley is fermented to produce this liqueur, which is common in Tibet and Qinghai.

**Quanxing daqu** (*chwen-sing da-choo*) 全兴大曲 This sweet, refreshing liqueur is produced in Sichuan.

**Shuanggou daqu** (*shwang-go da-choo*) 双沟大曲 This product comes from Jiangsu, and has a strong, refreshing aroma.

**Wuliangye** (*woo-liang-yeh*) 五粮液 Made from five different cereals, this is one of the most common and popular liqueurs in China. It is produced in Sichuan, in the city of Yibing.

**Yanghe daqu** (*yang-heh da-choo*) 羊河大曲 Made from barley, wheat and black soya, this liqueur is typical of Jiangsu. It has an alcohol content of up to 48 percent proof.

**Zhuyeqing** (*joo-yeh-ching*) 竹叶青 This classic liqueur is flavored with bamboo leaves. It is popular throughout China.

BEVERAGES

## RICE WINES

Traditional Chinese rice wine (mijiu, *mee-jioh*) is made by fermenting sugared glutinous rice. It is fairly high in alcohol (15-20 percent proof), amber-colored, and has a distinctive taste, which is dry or sweet depending on the type. There are five kinds of rice wine, each one resulting from a different kind of rice and production process: *yuanhongjiu* (dry), *jiafanjiu* (medium-dry), *sanniangjiu* (medium-sweet), *xiangxuejiu* (sweet, like Port) and *hongqujiu*, made from red rice and produced in central and eastern China in particular.

Rice wine is consumed in small quantities, cold or warm, at festivals and banquets. It is frequently used in cooking, both for preparing dishes and in sauces and marinades. Its medicinal properties (it stimulates the circulation and relaxes the muscles) have been recognized since ancient times, when it was considered "the best medicine of all".

**Guihuajiu** (*gweh-hwa-jioh*) 桂花酒 Rice wine aromatized with osmanthus flowers. It is moderately alcoholic (13 percent proof).

**Shaoxingjiu** (*shao-sing-jioh*) 绍 兴 酒 Known also as "huangjiu" (*hwang-jioh*, yellow wine), this liqueur-like rice wine is similar to dry sherry. Produced in the homonymous area in Zhejiang, it is left to age in terracotta vases for at least ten years (the most superior product ages for 40). It has been around since ancient times, and today it is still very popular, especially in the south of China. It is drunk tepid, at a temperature of 35-40 degrees, in special

# BEVERAGES

glasses. The most celebrated kind of rice wine, it is used particularly for toasts at banquets and festivals.

## GRAPE WINES
In recent years, China has entered into partnership with France to produce grape wines on Chinese soil. The results have been positive. Generally speaking, the wines are liqueur-like and low in alcohol. The following entries refer to the production houses and not to the individual wines, which in Chinese do not have their own names but are simply referred to according to their characteristics (for example *Sweet white wine, Red grape wine, Special brandy*, etc.).
In China it is not customary to drink different wines with different foods.

**Changchen** (*chang-chen*) 长 城 The Great Wall of China. This estate produces low-alcohol white wines that are sweet and liqueur-like.

**Kuihua** (*kweh-hwa*) 葵花 Sunflower. This production house turns out sweet, white and red wines, brandy and vermouth.

**Wangchao** (*wang-chao*) 王朝 Dynasty. Sino-French partnership with headquarters in Tianjing, producing red and white wines.

**Yeguangbei** (*yeh-gwang-bay*) 夜光杯 Glass that shines with the moon. This producer makes red wines and a special kind of brandy.

## Beer

Beer (pijiu, *pee-jioh*) is the second most popular beverage in China after tea. Qingdao is the most well-known brand and is also exported into the West. It takes its name from the homonymous city in Shandong where the Germans established a concession and – to get over their homesickness – a brewery. Other famous beers are Wuxing, Zhonghua and Sankong ("the three Confucius"), not to mention the *special beer* from Beijing (Beijing tezhong pijiu, *bay-jing te-joong pee-jioh*) and from Shanghai (Shanghai tezhong pijiu, *shang-hai te-joong pee-jioh*). Chinese beer is widely available, cheap, and has a delicate taste and low alcohol content (between 2,9 and 3,5 proof). It is drunk mainly at mealtimes, from breakfast to dinner. Large supermarkets and luxury hotels also sell foreign beer – mostly German – at a very high price. The Tibetans drink a beer made from barley called "chang" (*chang*).

# CONDIMENTS AND MAIN INGREDIENTS

The Chinese have been using oil, salt, sugar, rice wine and other spices in cooking since the second millennium BC. Chinese chefs have always been masters at bringing out the flavor of dishes through the precise combination of simple ingredients and in the knowledgeable use of spices and aromatic plants. Nothing is left to chance: every ingredient has its proper place, having to nourish and strengthen the body, draw the eye and stimulate the gastric juices.

**Chinese vinegar** (cu, *tsoo*) Made from rice wine, this is sweeter than wine vinegar. Red vinegar from Zhejiang is the best.

**Cornstarch** (yumifen, *yoo-mee-fen*) Used to flour meat before cooking so that it stays tender and acquires an aroma. Cornstarch is also used as a thickener in sauces and to prepare sweets: the semi-transparent sheets that wrap numerous Chinese sweets are made from lard, cornstarch and hot water.

**Aniseed** (bajiao, *ba-jiao*) Aromatic plant of the Magnolia family. The seeds, which have a distinctive eight-pointed shape and a subtle aroma that is reminiscent of liquorice, are used, often in conjunction with other spices.

**Water chestnuts** (lizi, *lee-ds*) These are the small, dark fruit of a plant that grows in water, and are crunchy and slightly sweet in taste. The canned variety is peeled and light in color.

**Chinese cabbage** (baicai, *bai-tsai*) Known also as Beijing cabbage or celery cabbage because of its compact, elongated shape and yellowish-white leaves. More delicate in flavor than our own varieties, Chinese cabbage is now to be found in many markets.

**Chinese dates** (zaozi, *dsao-ds*) Smaller and sweeter than the African variety, Chinese dates are bright red in color.

**Spring onion** (chuncong, *choon-tsong*) This delicate and fresh-tasting plant has a small bulb and long, thin leaves. Not unlike garlic, its flavor is more intense than that of spring onions over here. It is a basic ingredient in Chinese cuisine, representing the *yin* pole (see **Cuisine and medicine**, p. 35), and it is always used in conjunction with its *yang* complement, ginger.

**Lily flowers** (baihehua, *bai-heh-hwa*) Dried tiger-lily flowers. They have a delicate aroma, similar to musk.

**Lotus leaves** (heye, *heh-yeh*) Lotus leaves are used to wrap food before steaming, so giving it their distinctive and delicate aroma. The small "parcels" are served whole and opened with chopsticks.

**Chinese mushrooms** (mogu, *moh-goo*) The most common type is the *winter mushroom* (Lentinus edodes, in Chinese "donggu", *doong-goo*), so-called because harvested during the cold season. These small, dark mushrooms are sold dry and are reconstituted in water for 15-20 minutes before cooking. They have a flat, circular cap and a fibrous stalk, which is not used. Other varieties that feature in Chinese cooking include the *straw mushroom* (Volvariella volvacea, in Chinese "caogu", *tsao-goo*) and *little Judas' ears* (Auricularia auricula-judae), known in China as *ears of wood* (muer, *moo-er*) or *ears of cloud* (yuner, *yoon-er*); found growing on tree trunks, they are small and curly and dark grey in color, and have a delicate flavor. The *caterpillar grass* mushroom (chongcao, *chong-tsao* – Cordyceps chinensis) is used for its curative properties.

**Bamboo shoots** (sun, *soon*; zhusun, *joo-soon*) These are the small, delicate shoots that form at the base of this priceless plant, which in China is used in all manner of ways (from scaffolding to sleeping mats, soup tureens to piping supplies of water to the fields for irrigation). They are harvested twice a year, in summer and in winter; the shoots that are gathered in winter are the best. They have a sweetish flavor and a slightly crisp consistency. Canned bamboo shoots are available from exotic food stores.

**Beansprouts** (douya, *doe-ya*) Green soya (mung beans) are allowed to germinate and the shoots are gathered once they have reached a height of six-seven centimeters. They are sweet and tender and are easy to grow at home.

**Chili oil** (lajiao you, *la-jiao yo*) Vegetable oil aromatized with chili pepper. It is used abundantly in the south-west of China.

**Peanut oil** (huasheng you, *hwa-sheng yo*) This, and sunflower oil, are the standard cooking oils.

**Sesame oil** (zhima you, *jr-ma yo*) This very aromatic oil is made from sesame seeds. It is used in small quantities as a condiment, especially in the south of China.

**Sweet soya paste** (tianmian jiang, *tien-mien jiang*) Made from yellow soya, rice flour and sugar, this delicate sauce is used prevalently in cuisine in Beijing.

**Sichuan pepper** (huajiao, *hwa-jiao*) Known also as Chinese red pepper, this spice does not in fact belong to the pepper family. It is a reddish-brown berry that grows in Sichuan. Roasted and ground, it gives dishes a spicy aroma that is a cross between the taste of pepper and the sour twang of citrus peel.

**Five-spice powder** (wuxiang fen, *woo-siang fen*) Aromatic blend obtained by grinding fennel, cloves, aniseed, cinnamon and Sichuan pepper.

**Lotus roots** (lian-peng, *lien-peng*) Similar to American potatoes, lotus roots are elongated and have a diameter of five-six centimeters. In the West they come in distinctive circular slices with eight holes that are dried or vacuum-packed. The Chinese eat the root fresh; seasoned with ginger juice and sesame oil it makes a pleasant appetizer.

# CONDIMENTS AND MAIN INGREDIENTS

**Rice** (dami, *da-mee*) Circular, elongated or glutinous, rice forms the basis of every Chinese meal: an ancient proverb says that "a meal without rice is like a beautiful woman without an eye". Rice is rinsed several times before it is cooked (Confucius said that it should always be white and clean). It can be served plain (in which case it takes on the flavor of the different dishes), or stir-fried together with meat, shrimps, eggs and vegetables. Rice cooked slowly to form a soft, almost liquid substance is the staple breakfast dish in China. Glutinous rice (nianmi, *nien-mee*) is rich in starch and it is for this reason that it is so thick; it is used in sweets and as a filling. The rice crust (guoba, *gwoba*) that forms at the bottom of the pan during cooking is fried and served with soup much as croutons are here. Rice flour is used to make noodles, sweets and beverages.

**Sweet and sour sauce** (tiansuan jiang, *tien-swan jiang*) This rather dense sauce is characteristically sweet and sour at the same time. It is made from tomato pulp, corn syrup, sugar, pineapple, vinegar and cornstarch.

**Fish-flavored sauce** (yuxiang you, *yoo-siang yo*) This sauce is made from fermented soya, garlic, sugar, ginger and rice wine. Its unusual method of preparation gives the sauce a distinctive and delicate flavor.

**Sweet bean sauce** (hongdou sha, *hong-doe sha*) This thick, dark red sauce made from azuki beans, sugar and spices is vaguely reminiscent of chestnut purée. It is frequently used as a filling in sweets (even if it isn't very sweet), but it also features in many savory dishes.

**Spicy bean sauce** (ladouban jiang, *la-doe-ban jiang*) A thick sauce made from yellow or black soya, to which garlic and chili pepper are added.

**Oyster sauce** (haoyou, *hao-yo*) This condiment is made from oyster extract, sugar and soya, and is frequently used in the Shanghai and Canton areas. The taste of fish vanishes during fermentation, leaving a very delicate flavor.

**Sesame sauce** (majiang, *ma-jiang*) This thick sauce made from sesame seeds is rich and substantial and tastes a bit like peanut butter.

**Soy sauce** (Jiangyou, *jiang-yo*) With a history that goes back to ancient times, soy sauce is one of the basic ingredients in Chinese cuisine, and of Asian cuisine in general. Fermented soya and roasted cereals (usually rice, but wheat and barley are also used) are combined; the aroma and consistency of the resulting sauce depends on the time that the mixture is left to soak. The most common varieties are "shengchou wang" (*sheng-cho wang*, light soy sauce), which is ideal for use with fish and in delicate dishes that must not change color, and "laochou wang" (*lao-cho wang*, dark soy sauce), which is more suitable for meat dishes and slow cooked recipes.

**Soy sauce with mushrooms** (caogu laochou, *tsao-goo lao-*

*cho*) Soy sauce aromatized with the delicate and subtle-tasting *straw mushroom.*

**Spicy soy sauce** (lajiang, *la-jiang*) Spicy sauce with a complex flavor that is difficult to describe. It is made from soya, sesame oil, Sichuan pepper and various spices.

**Hoisin sauce** (haixianjiang, *hai-sien-jiang*) This thick sauce reputedly tastes of "the sea". It is dark red and has a bitter-sweet flavor. It is made by combining fermented soya with sugar, flour, garlic, chili pepper, rice wine, vinegar and sesame oil. In southern China remember to use the Cantonese pronunciation, *hoy-sin-jion.*

**Red sauce** (hongyou, *hong-yo*) Made from soya, rice wine and sugar, this sauce is typically used in the cuisine of Shanghai. It gives dishes an attractive dark red color.

**Sesame** (zhima, *jr-ma*) The small seeds (light or dark) of this plant are roasted lightly and used to aromatize numerous dishes and to make sauces and sweets.

**Chinese noodles** (mian, *mien*) Chinese noodles can be made from wheat flour, rice flour or green soya. What matters is that they are long, since long noodles are synonymous with long life. Noodles made from wheat – to which egg is sometimes added – also come in thin, flat strips (miantiao, *mien-tiao*) and take only three-four minutes to cook. Noodles made from rice or soya (mifen, *mee-fen*) take even less time to cook; they need to be immersed in boiling water only very briefly and becomes gelatinous on cooking. The debate about who invented noodles (the Chinese or the Italians?) is ongoing, but it is worth remembering that Chinese noodles have a different consistency to Italian spaghetti and don't go down well with people who like their pasta *al dente*.

**Tofu** (doufu, *toefoo*) Commonly known as soya cheese, tofu is made from the coagulated liquid that results when yellow soya is soaked. It is highly nutritious and for this reason forms the basis of the diet not only of the Chinese but of all Asian people: it is rich in natural lechithins, contains a modest amount of protein (about 12 percent), minerals and vitamins, and has a low fat content. It is very versatile and lends itself to various dishes. It is supplied fresh, in cakes, but it can also be stored in a number of different ways: dry (doufugan, *toefoo-gan*), fermented (doufuru, *toefoo-roo*), in sheets or strips, or in a gelatin mold – *brain of tofu* or *tofu-brain* (doufunao, *toefoo-nao*). There is also the so-called *stinking tofu* (choudoufu, *cho-toefoo*).

**Rice wine.** See **Beverages**, p. 23.

**Ginger** (shengjiang, *sheng-jiang*) The root of this plant is one of the basic ingredients in Chinese cuisine. It has a distinctive flavor that is bitter and spicy and yet delicate all at once. Thought to represent the *yang* pole (see **Cuisine and medicine**, p. 35), it is always used in conjunction with its *yin* complement, spring onion. The "young" root, deriving from a plant of no more than a year, is often pickled and served as an appetizer: it is only slightly spicy and stimulates the appetite, preparing the stomach for digestion. The root of older plants is stronger, and is grated, sliced or pressed and added to food during cooking to flavor it and make it more digestible.

# CUISINE AND MEDICINE

In Chinese culture, the universe is animated by two opposite and complementary principles, *yin* and *yang*, which between them give life to all things. *Yin* is night, winter, water, femininity, passivity; *yang* is day, summer, fire, masculinity, activity. In reality nothing is all *yin* or all *yang*; every being contains both elements in varying degrees; and it is from the dynamic balance between the two that every reality comes into being.

This frame of reference also applies to the diet: there are *yang* foods (meat, fried and fatty food and canned foods) and *yin* foods (crustaceans, vegetables, fruit, boiled food and dishes that are steamed). Balance between the two principles within the meal, as in any single dish, is the basic rule for health; contrarily, excess of one or the other leads to imbalance and sickness.

Chinese doctors and philosophers have always been interested in the relationship between diet and physical well-being, in particular in relation to immortality (this is a real obsession) and the maintenance of good health in old age.

Dietetics is an important branch of traditional Chinese medicine and is the first stage in treatment. The curative properties of many foodstuffs such as Chinese dates, sesame, sweet potatoes, ginger, some varieties of mushroom, etc. have been known since ancient times. Importance was also given to the amount of food eaten and to the way in which it was consumed. These observations foregrounded modern nutritional science.

The following are made from ingredients which, in

addition to giving the dishes their pleasant aroma, also have salutary and medicinal properties.

**Bagua tang** (*ba-gwa tang*) 八卦汤 Turtle soup. Thin slices of turtle are stir-fried with ginger and spring onion and then cooked slowly in broth together with *caterpillar grass* mushrooms.

**Dongchong kaoya** (*doong-chong kao-ya*) 冬虫烤鸭 Whole boiled duck stuffed with *caterpillar grass* mushrooms and stewed slowly with ginger, spring onion and rice wine.

**Huaqishen dongchongcao dun ruge** (*hwa-chee-shen doong-chong-tsao doon roo-ge*) 花旗参冬虫草炖乳鸽 Stewed pigeon with ginseng, *caterpillar grass* mushrooms and Chinese lychees (white-colored berries).

**Mizao yangrou** (*mee-dsao yang-ro*) 蜜枣羊肉 Small pieces of mutton are stir-fried and then steamed on a layer of lotus pods together with candied dates filled with orange peel. The ingredients are placed on a serving dish and smothered with warm honey.

All over China, in the towns and in the country, in the markets and on the roadside, there are stalls selling a vast selection of *dim sum*, or snacks, which are often prepared on the spot. Ravioli, hand-made noodles, fritters and steamed filled rolls are common in the north of China, while in the south you will find "shaomai" (*shao-mai*, circular ravioli), "zongzi" (*dsoong-ds*, lotus leaf "parcels" filled with rice), "yuanxiao" (*ywen-siao*, balls made from glutinous rice flour filled with various ingredients), the familiar spring rolls (chunjuan, *choon-jwan*) and wonton (*hoon-doon*), and other specialties.

The term *dim sum* (in Mandarin dianxin, *dien-sin*) means *little heart* or *heart-toucher*, in the sense of "something that goes straight to the heart". This might conceivably be a reference to the delicious fillings that they conceal, or to the way in which they delight the palate and stimulate the imagination. *Dim sum* come in numerous forms (ravioli, small bundles, tiny breads and parcels filled with all manner of ingredients) and are cooked in various ways (fried, boiled or steamed). The traditional snacks that go with tea are eaten at all hours of the day or night.

*Dim sum* are also served in restaurants, but only for breakfast or lunch. There is no need to ask for the menu – the *dim sum* arrive on trolleys designed especially to keep them hot. These are wheeled by elegant waitresses who are meant to list their contents in sweet song, but who tend rather to shout aggressively. Customers serve themselves straight from the trolley. The Chinese customarily eat *dim sum* in crowded, noisy restaurants, particularly at lunch on Sundays: this is a pleasant social ritual.

**Baozi** (*bao-ds*) 包子 Round rolls containing chicken, spring onion, ginger and bamboo shoots, steamed on cabbage leaves. They are very common throughout China, and make the mid-morning or afternoon snack *par excellence*.

**Bingtang hulu** (*bing-tang hoo-loo*) 冰糖葫芦 Small, cherry-sized round fruits that are threaded onto a stick and covered in caramel.

**Chao hundun** (*chao hoon-doon*) 炒馄饨 Better known by their Cantonese name (wonton), these are small bundles made from a flour, water and egg mixture, which contain pork, shrimps, ginger and spring onion. They are fried and served with a sweet and sour sauce made from tomato, orange juice, sugar, rice wine, soy sauce and sesame oil.

**Chunjuan** (*choon-jwan*) 春卷 *Spring rolls*. This famous dish appears on Chinese menus all over the world but is often nothing like the original. In fact the filling is traditionally much more elaborate and there are numerous kinds: pork, mushrooms and bamboo shoots, or shrimps and beansprouts, to name but two. Vegetarian spring rolls contain carrots, Chinese cabbage and other vegetables.

**Dansu baozi** (*dan-soo bao-ds*) 蛋 素包 子 Steamed circular ravioli made from an egg-based dough, containing mushrooms, bamboo shoots, runner beans, ginger and spring onion.

**Guotie jiao** (*gwo-tieh jiao*) 锅贴饺 Ravioli filled with shrimps, pork, ginger and spring onion, which are first stir-fried and then boiled.

**Hongyou shuijiao** (*hong-yo shweh-jiao*) 红油水饺 Half moon-shaped ravioli made from a flour-water mixture and containing pork, spring onion and ginger.
They are boiled and served with a sauce made from soya, sugar, rice wine, garlic, chili pepper and sesame oil. The variety found in Sichuan are particularly tasty.

**Hundun tang** (*hoon-doon tang*) 馄饨汤 *Wonton* soup (see **Chao hundun**, p. 38). *Wonton* filled with pork and shrimps are cooked in a broth of chicken and spring onion. The Shanghai variety is excellent.

**Jiaozi** (*jiao-ds*) 饺子 Generic term referring to half moon-shaped ravioli irrespective of their filling and the way that they are cooked.
In the north of China *Jiaozi* are traditionally eaten at New Year to invoke good fortune: in fact the half-moon shape is reminiscent of the "yuanbao" (*ywen-bao*), a small gold or silver ingot used in ancient times as currency. The entire family gathers for the occasion to prepare them: it is an opportunity to spend time together and chat.

**Jizhou** (*jee-jo*) 鸡粥 Soup made from glutinous rice, chicken cut into very thin strips and egg white.

# DIM SUM

**Mahua** (*ma-hwa*) 麻花 Plaited, circular cake with a hole in the center, made from sesame, hazelnuts, sugar and vanilla. Reputed to stay fresh and crunchy for 100 days, it is a specialty of Tianjin.

**Mantou** (*man-toe*) 馒头 White, rubbery steamed rolls made from wheat flour. In China the practice of keeping them in plastic bags makes them more rubbery still.

**Shaobing** (*shao-bing*) 烧饼 Fried sweet garnished with sesame seeds.

**Shaomai** (*shao-mai*) 烧卖 Sack-shaped ravioli left open at the top and steamed. They contain shrimps, bamboo shoots and Chinese cabbage, and are flavored with rice wine and sesame oil.

**Wandouzhou** (*wan-doe-jo*) 豌豆粥 Pea soup typical of Beijing. Apparently it was invented by a cook named Zhao who subsequently took the nickname Zhao Pea.

**Xianbing** (*sien-bing*) 馅饼 Generic term referring to fritters with a variety of fillings (chicken, vegetables, shrimps, etc.)

**Xierou jiao** (*sie-ro jiao*) 蟹肉饺 Fried ravioli made from an egg-based dough, containing crab meat, egg, ginger and spring onion.

**Youbing** (*yo-bing*) 油饼 Generic term referring to the fritters made at road-side kiosks in large, blackened, sizzling pans. Don't be put off by the apparent lack of hygiene: the boiling oil kills all germs...

**Youtiao** (*yo-tiao*) 油条 Fried bread that is elongated in shape and has a spongy consistency.

**Yuanxiao** (*ywen-siao*) 元宵 These sweets are traditionally eaten at the Lantern Festival. Balls made from glutinous rice flour are filled with a variety of ingredients: sweet bean sauce, black sesame, Chinese dates, prunes, almonds. One kind (tangyuan, *tang-ywen*) is boiled in a syrup of water and sugar and served in separate bowls. They are also known as "futuanzi" (*foo-twan-ds*, floating balls). Because of their glueyness they symbolize family unity and the joy of being together. The shape of these sweets is called "tuan" (*twan*), which also means *hug*, and their rotund structure is "yuan" (*ywen*), meaning *to gather*.

**Yuebing** (*yweh-bing*) 月饼 *Moon biscuits*. These sweets are traditionally eaten at the autumn festival of the full moon. They are made from a dough that is similar to shortcrust pastry and contain a variety of sweet and savory fillings including meat, soya, vegetables, almonds, coconut, cooked Chinese ham, sweet bean sauce and egg yolk. The circular shape represents the full moon and, metaphorically speaking, the unification of the family that is celebrated at this time. "Yuebing" can measure up to 40 cm in diameter and are decorated with drawings inspired by the various legends associated with the festival.

**Zhagao** (*ja-gao*) 炸糕 Generic term referring to fried sweets that are thin and crisp.

**Zongzi** (*dsoong-ds*) 粽子 Triangular "parcels" made from lotus leaves, containing glutinous rice and various sweet and savory ingredients. Traditionally eaten at the Dragon-Boat Festival. They can be filled with cooked Chinese ham, sugar and rice wine, or with pieces of chicken or duck, egg yolk and mushrooms, or even with sweet bean sauce, sesame, Chinese dates and candied fruit.

# CHINESE CUISINE IN THE WEST

Chinese cuisine has been available in the West for a number of years, and today it is served in many places, from sit-down restaurants to take-away joints. These are almost all family-run and offer modest prices. Unfortunately, these two characteristics are often linked to a third, less positive aspect: the absence of professional chefs – not to mention of other specialists typically found in the kitchen of restaurants in China: the person who chops the ingredients, the person who prepares the *dim sum*, etc. This has resulted in the evolution of a poor-quality, hybrid cuisine. On the other hand, the cost of hiring specialized personnel is too great for many Chinese restaurant-owners; in China everybody knows how to cook, at least to some degree, and if you cook for yourself, why shouldn't you cook for others as well? Of course in this way the quality of the food is compromised, but the economic benefits for the restaurateurs – and by extension for their customers – cannot be ignored. Who's complaining, after all? Chinese cuisine – like all "exported" cuisines – has changed in conformity to local tastes. The food that is to be found in the West is often very different from traditional gastronomy. This is partly for practical reasons, such as the difficulty of getting hold of ingredients, the lack of good cooks and the need to keep costs down. However, it is also the result of the deliberate attempt by the restaurant concerned to "bridge the gap" between two very different sets of tastes.

The cuisine in China uses fresh ingredients but these

rarely appear in Chinese restaurants in the West, as
much for practical and economic reasons as because
they are objectively difficult to come by. One
fundamental difference lies in the way the food is eaten
and in the order in which the dishes are brought to the
table. For example, while in China soup is drunk
throughout the meal (often with noisy slurps that in no
way conflict with the Chinese code of manners), and tea
only at the end, here we order soup at the beginning as
an appetizer, drink tea with the meal, finish with a sweet
and woe if we leave without coffee at the very end!
Moreover, the table is set in western style (often there
are not even chopsticks), and the dishes are served on
separate plates rather than from communal dishes at the
center of the table (see **The Chinese table**, p. 8), from
which the Chinese help themselves with their
chopsticks (Westerners travelling in China are often
horrified by this custom). In this way, the conviviality
and collective enjoyment of a good meal, which is so
important in China, is lost.
The menu is compiled on the basis of customers'
preferences and their tastes can also result in the
alteration of traditional recipes. Chicken-based dishes
are more common than dishes with pork; fried food
appears more often than food that is boiled or steamed;
plain white rice is often superseded by stir-fried rice
("Cantonese", but a person from Canton would struggle
to recognize it); and dishes containing unconventional
meat – eternal symbols of the originality and creative
genius of Chinese gastronomy – are excluded. In the

same way tofu, which does not find favor with the western palate, is rare (and often canned), even though in China it is a protagonist of hundreds of recipes. Moreover, the use of condiments and strong spices is limited, and priority is given to gravies and "juices", which are thickened with cornstarch and flavored with monosodium glutamate. This substance is frequently blamed for the well-known "Chinese restaurant syndrome"; however, it must be said that in no way is it typical of Chinese cuisine, where flavors are brought out through skilful combinations and contrasts.

Unfortunately, glutamate is often used by unprofessional cooks without a passion for food, who do not know how to bring out the flavors of the ingredients naturally - and who, moreover, ride on the back of their customers' basic ignorance.

The perfect example of this transformation is *chicken with almonds* (in Chinese *gongbao jiding*, chicken of the deputy king), perhaps the most well-known Chinese dish in the world. In preparing this dish the spicy condiment is eliminated and almonds are used instead of peanuts as in the original recipe (it goes without saying that ginger and spring onion are nowhere to be seen). It is undoubtedly a tasty dish but one that is foreign to most Chinese people.

But there is no need to go all the way to Beijing to taste crispy duck, or to Shanghai to savor good spring rolls: many restaurants have a "double menu" (one for Chinese and one for other customers). Here you need only to make friends with the manager or the waiters and you will get a more "Chinese" treatment and taste typical dishes cooked according to traditional methods – the ones that the Chinese prepare for themselves.

DELICIOUS!

# COOKING METHODS

Chinese cuisine has its roots in rural areas and over the centuries it has had to reckon with famine and lack of resources. In the face of this, Chinese cooks have managed to make a virtue of necessity: in having to chop ingredients into small pieces (this is a very important operation, which can sometimes take as long as cooking the food itself) to reduce the cooking time and save fuel, they succeed in preserving their taste and nutritional content; by treating each aliment as a challenge and having only limited resources to hand, they manage to transform even the simplest ingredients into ever new delights. Marco Polo, who spent 17 years at the court of the Mongolian Emperor Kubilay, recognized the merits for which Chinese cuisine is now renowned: "there is no other cuisine in the world that succeeds in giving so much happiness with so little".

The preparation of the ingredients is vitally important and is the most time-consuming stage of cooking: vegetables, meat and fish must be chopped uniformly so that cooking is homogeneous. The Chinese cook everything: raw ingredients do not appear in dishes since they are considered difficult to digest – in fact the culinary art is referred to by the word "pengtiao" (*peng-tiao*), made up of "peng", meaning "to cook", and "tiao", which signifies "to harmonize" or "to match".

The most frequently-used implement in Chinese cooking is the wok (*wok*). This traditional concave iron frying pan, common throughout the Far East, allows food to be stir-fried, fried or stewed. Bamboo baskets can also be placed in the wok for easy steaming. The most common cooking

# COOKING METHODS

method involves stir-frying (chao, *chao*) the ingredients in a small quantity of very hot oil: in this way the meat is tender and juicy and the vegetables are slightly crisp. First the wok is set over the heat (add a drop of water to the pan and if it sizzles the wok is ready). The oil is then heated and the meat (or fish) is added and cooked for a few minutes only. After this, the contents are removed and the vegetables are cooked rapidly. Finally, the meat is returned to the pan together with the various seasonings and the ingredients are stirred for a few moments more to amalgamate the flavors. There are around 50 different methods of stir-frying.

Steaming is another popular method of cooking in China (zhengzhu, *jeng-joo*). It is used especially to make the infinite number of ravioli, tortelli and little parcels, but also to cook vegetables, fish, bread and sweets. The ingredients are placed in stackable bamboo baskets and set over a pan of boiling water. The steam rises through the bamboo fibers, cooking large quantities of food at the same time. In this way the use of fatty cooking oils is avoided and the flavors and consistency of the ingredients remain intact. In the south of China food is often wrapped in lotus leaves to keep it tender and so that it absorbs the delicate aroma of the plant.

In some recipes the ingredients have to be fried quickly (zha, *ja*); in this case the amount of oil and its temperature are greater. Meat and fish are fried in a light batter, usually made from egg and cornstarch, which forms a crisp coating, then the vegetables and condiments are added. Only a few, unusual recipes are complicated and take a long time to prepare. These often involve the use of different cooking methods at the same time. Examples are *Beijing crispy duck*, which is basted with a sugar-based sauce and baked repeatedly, the Cantonese *golden piglet*, which is roasted for a whole day, and two dishes from Sichuan: *smoked duck with tea and camphor*, which is marinated, steamed and smoked over a camphor wood fire, and *pig that returns to the pan*, which is boiled and then stir-fried. In the Guangdong area a technique called "cha siu" (in Mandarin chashao, *cha-shao*) is used for pork in particular; the method involves marinating the finely sliced meat in a mixture of soy sauce, rice wine, garlic, honey and ginger juice and then briefly cooking it in a very hot oven on a specially designed spit: the high temperature turns the sauce into a crispy coating.

# NATIONAL DISHES

Many typical regional dishes have been assimilated into national menus and are now common throughout China. However, there are numerous regional variations on every dish.

**Babao fan** (*ba-bao fan*) 八宝饭  Sweet typical of the Shanghai region. *Rice with eight treasures* is a pudding made from glutinous rice containing layers of nuts, Chinese dates and water chestnut purée, decorated with candied fruit and covered with sugar syrup. It is eaten on special occasions and at the Dragon-Boat Festival.

**Bainian jidan** (*bai-nien jee-dan*) 百年鸡蛋  *Eggs of the 100 years* are covered in a paste made from ash, salt, tea and quicklime and buried in the earth for 100 days. In this way the white of the egg takes on an amber color and the yolk becomes green. These delicate-tasting eggs keep for up to six months. An ancient recipe book makes the following suggestion: "While preparing the eggs, avoid strangers and keep contact with friends and acquaintances to a minimum; talk only if absolutely necessary".

**Bocaiban fensi** (*boh-tsai-ban fen-s*) 薄菜般粉丝  This cold dish is served as an appetizer. Boiled prawns are minced, seasoned with a generous amount of garlic and served on a plate of rice noodles.

**Chao doujiao** (*chao doe-jiao*) 炒豆角  Sugar-peas stir-fried with cashew nuts, spring onion, garlic, ginger and chili pepper, and seasoned with rice wine, soy sauce and a pinch of sugar.

**Chao sishu** or **Chao shucai** (*chao s-shoo* or *chao shoo-tsai*) 炒四蔬 or 炒蔬菜 Mix of four vegetables, finely chopped, stir-fried and seasoned with soy sauce. In general the dish comprises of carrots, bamboo shoots, mushrooms and beansprouts or broccoli.

**Congtou chao niurou** (*tsong-toe chao niu-ro*) 葱头炒牛肉 Beef cut into thin strips, cooked on the griddle and served with a thick sauce made from onions and pepper.

**Dandan mian** (*dan-dan mien*) 且且面 Noodles or thin strips of pasta seasoned with sesame sauce, chili pepper, ginger, spring onion and soy sauce, to which tiny pieces of fried pork and finely chopped peanuts are added. This dish, now served in all restaurants, originated in Sichuan as *dim sum*. It takes its name from the balance (*dan*) supporting all the items needed to knock together this dish – including the stove – which travelling food-sellers still carry on their shoulders.

**Doufu xiaren tang** (*toefoo sia-ren tang*) 豆腐虾仁汤 Soup made from tofu, shrimps, mushrooms, peas and cooked Chinese ham. It is very aromatic and somewhat gelatinous in consistency.

**Fanqie danhua tang** (*fan-chie dan-hwa tang*) 番茄蛋花汤 Soup made from lightly cooked tomatoes, tofu and eggs, flavored with garlic and ginger and garnished with spring onion. The eggs are beaten and poured in slowly to form attractive flower-like patterns. There is a variation on this dish that does not contain tofu.

**Gongbao jiding** (*goong-bao jee-ding*) 宫保鸡丁 Stir-fried chicken with peppers, peanuts and bamboo shoots, seasoned with chili pepper, garlic, ginger and spring onion. Originating in Sichuan but common all over China, this is the most renowned Chinese dish in the world, although it is more familiar as the variation *chicken with almonds*. The name, which in Chinese means *chicken of the deputy king*, was reputedly coined by an official during a banquet given by his superior in Chengdu in the 19th century.

**Gulao rou** (*goo-lao ro*) 古老肉 Sweet and sour pork. This traditional Cantonese dish meaning *old pork*, or *pork in ancient style*, features on Chinese menus all over the world. Small pieces of fried pork are stir-fried with peppers, bamboo and pineapple and seasoned with a bitter-sweet sauce made from vinegar, sugar, tomato, soya and sesame oil.

**Haoyou niurou** (*hao-yo niu-ro*) 好油牛肉 The recipe for this classic and flavorsome dish involves marinating small pieces of beef in a mixture of rice wine and oyster sauce. The meat is then stir-fried with broccoli, carrots, mushrooms and bamboo shoots and seasoned with ginger and spring onion.

**Hongshao yu** (*hong-shao yoo*) 红烧渔 This dish is typical

of the Shanghai region. The fish (usually red mullet, bass or carp) is fried whole and served with mushrooms, bamboo shoots and water chestnuts flavored with spring onion, ginger and garlic. The dish is dressed with a sweet and sour sauce made from soya, flour, rice wine, sugar and tomato.

**Jisi chaofan** (*jee-s chao-fan*) 鸡丝炒饭 Stir-fried rice with small pieces of chicken and a variety of vegetables (carrots, bamboo shoots, broccoli, beansprouts). It is very common abroad, especially in Great Britain and the United States.

**Jisi chaomian** (*jee-s chao-mien*) 鸡丝炒面 Stir-fried noodles with small pieces of chicken and a variety of vegetables (carrots, bamboo shoots, broccoli, beansprouts).

**Ji zhuo doufu** (*jee jwo toefoo*) 鸡啄豆腐 Tofu is crumbled and stir-fried together with tiny pieces of fried pork and coarsely ground peanuts; finely chopped mushrooms, lily flowers, bamboo and fresh onions are then added and the ingredients are seasoned with sesame oil. In Chinese this dish is called *cockerel that pecks at the tofu* because the pecking motion of a cockerel and the movement made to break up the tofu are similar.

**Liang dong** (*liang-doong*) 两冬 In Chinese this dish is called *the two winters*. Winter bamboo shoots (the most prized variety) and winter mushrooms (see **Condiments and main ingredients**, p. 27) are stir-fried and seasoned with soy sauce and sesame oil.

# NATIONAL DISHES

**Mala jiding** (*ma-la jee-ding*) 麻辣 鸡丁 Originating in Sichuan, this is a spicy dish with a strong flavor. Diced chicken is stir-fried with peppers, seasoned with soy sauce, sesame paste and chili pepper and garnished with sesame seeds.

**Mapo doufu** (*ma-poh toefoo*) 麻婆豆腐 This spicy classic dish from Sichuan is now eaten throughout China. It is believed to have been invented 400 years ago by one Grandma Chen, nicknamed *the pock-marked lady* (in fact the name of the dish means *tofu of the pock-marked old lady*), who owned a famous eatery in Chengdu. Cubes of tofu, pork and water chestnuts are cooked in a sauce made from chili pepper, garlic and sweet bean paste; at the end a generous sprinkling of freshly-ground Sichuan pepper is added.

**Mifan** (*mee-fan*) 米饭 White rice, king of the Chinese table. Its plain appearance and slightly rubbery consistency make it seem unappetizing, but it should be eaten alongside the other dishes and flavored with the different sauces.

**Mogu caixin** (*moh-goo tsai-sin*) 蘑菇菜心 Chinese cabbage and mushrooms, stir-fried and seasoned with sesame oil.

**Muxu rou** (*moo-soo ro*) 木须肉 Stir-fried pork with mushrooms, bamboo, dried lily flowers and beaten eggs.

**Niurou chaofan** (*niu-ro chao-fan*) 牛肉炒饭 Stir-fried rice with small pieces of beef and vegetables (carrots, bamboo shoots, broccoli, beansprouts).

# NATIONAL DISHES

**Niurou chaomian** (*niu-ro chao-mien*) 牛肉炒面
Stir-fried noodles with tiny pieces of beef and
vegetables (carrots, bamboo shoots, broccoli,
beansprouts).

**Qiang huanggua** (*chiang hwang-gwa*) 炝黄瓜 Finely
sliced cucumber stir-fried briefly in sesame oil with chili
pepper and Sichuan pepper. This dish is usually served as
an appetizer.

**Shaguo doufu** (*sha-gwo toefoo*) 沙锅豆腐 This dish
originated in Beijing. Tofu soup with mushrooms,
cabbage, cooked Chinese ham and shrimps. The
ingredients are cooked in a special terracotta pan

**Shucai chaofan** (*shoo-tsai chao-fan*) 蔬菜炒饭 Stir-fried
rice with vegetables, usually carrots, bamboo shoots,
mushrooms, broccoli and beansprouts.

**Shucai chaomian** (*shoo-tsai chao-mien*) 蔬菜炒面 Stir-
fried noodles with vegetables, usually carrots, bamboo
shoots, mushrooms, broccoli and beansprouts.

**Suanla luobo** (*swan-la lwo-boh*) 酸辣萝卜 Horseradish
and carrots are chopped into matchstick-sized lengths and
seasoned with ground ginger, sugar, vinegar and soy
sauce. The ingredients are stir-fried with chili pepper and
served with a dash of sesame oil, usually as an appetizer.
The combination of the different condiments gives the
vegetables a sweet and spicy flavor.

# NATIONAL DISHES

**Suanla tang** (*swan-la tan*) 酸辣汤 Very flavorsome soup made from small pieces of chicken, mushrooms, tofu, bamboo shoots and peas, and seasoned with rice wine, soy sauce and freshly ground pepper. These ingredients give the soup its typical sour and spicy flavor.

**Suantian tudousi** (*swan-tien too-doe-s*) 酸甜土豆丝 Potatoes cut into matchsticks are stir-fried together with Sichuan pepper, vinegar, soy sauce and sugar, and sprinkled with minced spring onion to serve. It is a tasty dish with a crisp consistency and the characteristic bitter-sweet taste.

**Suchao douya** (*soo-chao doe-ya*) 素炒豆芽 Stir-fried beansprouts seasoned with sesame oil.

**Tangcu daxia** (*tang-tsoo da-sia*) 糖醋大虾 Fried prawns served with a sweet and sour sauce made from rice wine, soy sauce, sugar, spring onion and ginger.

**Tangcu yu** (*tang-tsoo yoo*) 糖醋渔 Fried fish in a sweet and sour sauce with peppers and pineapple.

**Wuxiang xunyu** (*woo siang soon-yoo*) 五香熏鱼 Fillets of fish (usually trout or sole) marinated in rice wine and fried lightly, then stir-fried together with ginger, spring onion and five-spice powder (see **Condiments and main ingredients**, p. 29).

**Xiangsuji** (*siang-soo-jee*) 香酥鸡 Fried chicken with a crisp batter coating.

# NATIONAL DISHES

**Xiaren tang** (*sia-ren tang*) 虾仁汤 Thick soup made from prawn pulp and grains of corn. Egg white, ginger and cornstarch are added. It is served with a spring onion garnish.

**Xihongshi chao dan** (*see-hong-shr chao dan*) 西红柿炒蛋 Scrambled eggs with stir-fried tomatoes, ginger and spring onion.

**Yumi tang** (*yoo-mee tang*) 玉米汤 Thick corn soup. One recipe uses crab meat and another uses tofu.

**Zhengzhu rouwan** (*jeng-joo ro-wan*) 蒸猪肉丸 Meatballs made from pork and water chestnuts. They are seasoned with ginger and spring onion, rolled in glutinous rice and steamed, and served on cabbage leaves.

**Zhusi chaofan** (*joo-s chao-fan*) 猪丝炒饭 Stir-fried rice with small pieces of pork and vegetables, usually carrots, bamboo shoots, mushrooms, broccoli and beansprouts.

**Zhusi chaomian** (*joo-s chao-mien*) 猪丝炒面 Stir-fried noodles with small pieces of pork and vegetables, usually carrots, bamboo shoots, mushrooms, broccoli and beansprouts.

# REGIONAL DISHES

Chinese cooking is traditionally divided into four distinct geographical areas on the basis of the physical environment and climatic conditions: the area of Beijing and Shandong in the north; the region of Canton and Guangxi in the south; Shanghai, Fujian and Zhejidang to the east; and Sichuan to the west. In summary, the cuisine in the north makes generous use of soy sauce and is celebrated for its ravioli, noodles and crispy duck, while in the south, rice and sweet, delicate flavors are predominant; around Shanghai, fish, sweet and sour dishes and soups hold sway, while in the west, hot, spicy dishes prevail. The Chinese have a very expeditious way of describing their complex culinary art: "Savory in the north, sweet in the south, spicy in the west, sour in the east".

## BEIJING

In the northern provinces of China the climate is harsh for most of the year. The prevalent crops are therefore cereals that can withstand the severe winters and dry summers (barley, wheat and maize), and vegetables that are easy to store, such as turnips, cabbage and sweet potatoes. This explains why people in the north of China eat large quantities of ravioli, noodles, steamed bread and focaccia, rather than rice. Lamb and mutton are the most common meats (this is due to the influence of nearby Mongolia) and the most frequently used condiment is soy sauce. Beijing and Xian have been capitals of the Chinese empire for many centuries and today the culinary art of the area encapsulates the refinement of the imperial cuisine and the ability of the rural people to satisfy their hunger with very little. The renowned Beijing crispy duck (Beijing kaoya) is exemplary of the elegance and ritual that once accompanied dishes from this region.

**Beijing kaoya** (*bay-jing kao-ya*) 北京烤鸭  The Chinese are masters in the art of cooking duck, which is the main dish on special occasions. This dish, famous throughout the world, is slow and laborious to prepare. The end result is a bird with an attractive, deep red, crispy coating. The ceremony with which it is served is also reminiscent of the imperial court: once it has come out of the oven, the chef displays the duck for the ritual compliments then, to the consternation of the table guests, he disappears into the kitchen carrying the fruit of his labors and the object of praise in his teeth. But never fear: no sooner has the masterpiece been cut into a few dozen pieces than it is once again on the table. At this point, each person takes a piece, dips it into a sauce made from sweet soya paste and places it on a thin pancake made from flour and water (bao bing, *bao bing*) together with a few strands of fresh spring onion; finally the precious delicacy is rolled up and is ready to be tasted (of course everything is done using chopsticks). The carcass is used to make soup, which is usually served later in the meal.

**Chuanyangrou tang** (*chwan-yang-ro tang*) 川羊肉汤
Cucumber and lamb soup. The meat is cut into thin strips

and marinated in soy sauce and sesame oil, seasoned with
fresh pepper and rice wine. Chinese cucumbers measure 40-
50 cm in length and are thin and more solid than our own.

**Congyou bing** (*tsong-yo bing*) 葱 油 饼 Round, flat bread
cooked on the griddle. The dough is made from cornmeal,
lard, fresh onions and coarse salt.

**Feicui fan** (*fay-tsweh fan*) 翡翠饭 Stir-fried rice with
Chinese cabbage and omelet cut into thin strips, garnished
with spring onion. In their fervent imagination, the Chinese
think that these ingredients give the rice the reflections and
color of jade – hence the name of the dish, *jade flower rice*.

**Huanghe liyu** (*hwang-heh lee-yoo*) 黄河鲤鱼 *Yellow
River carp* is first dipped in a batter mixture of water, flour
and cornstarch and browned, then it is stir-fried with a
sauce made from sugar, rice vinegar, soy sauce and rice
wine.

**Huocai daimao** (*hwo-tsai dai-mao*) 和菜戴帽 In Chinese
this dish is called *mixed dish with hat*. Small pieces of
pork, rice noodles and mixed vegetables (Chinese
cabbage, mushrooms, bamboo shoots and beansprouts)
are stir-fried. The dish is served covered with an omelet,
prepared separately.

**Jingjiang rousi** (*jing-jiang ro-s*) 京酱肉丝 Fine strips of
pork are floured, seasoned with soy sauce and stir-fried.
They are then stir-fried a second time with *sauce of the*

*capital* (jingjiang, *jing-jiang*), a condiment made from sweet bean sauce, sugar, soy sauce, sesame oil and rice wine.

**Shandong ya** (*shang-doong ya*) 山东鸭 Typical dish from Shandong. Stir-fried duck that has been marinated whole in a composite of rice wine, coriander, aniseed, pepper, soy sauce, spring onion and ginger. It is then steamed and finally it is cut into pieces and served cold with a sauce made from garlic, chili pepper, sugar, sesame oil and rice wine.

**Shuanyangrou** (*shwan-yang-ro*) 涮羊肉 *Mongolian fondu* is the convivial dish *par excellence*. It is typically eaten in the cold season and is served in a characteristic saucepan with a central cone filled with burning coal. The pan contains broth made from vegetables, rice noodles and tofu, which is kept at boiling point. Morsels of meat are dipped into the broth and cooked rapidly, then eaten together with a small quantity of vegetables and noodles from the pan and the various condiments to hand (soy sauce with minced spring onion and peanut oil; rice wine and ginger; sesame sauce and sesame oil; chili oil; rice wine and ground coriander... the list could go on). The ingredients and the broth are topped up little by little. Finally what remains of the broth is served. This dish apparently has its origins in the custom of the nomadic people of Mongolia of gathering around the fire in the evenings. They would cook raw food by rapidly immersing it in water heated in upturned iron helmets, and drink the restorative soup at the end.

**Shuijing xiaren** (*shweh-jing sia-ren*) 水晶虾仁 This dish is delicate both in substance and in name, which means *crystal prawns*. Prawns are dipped in batter made from flour, egg, rice wine and sugar, and stir-fried together with peas, ginger and spring onion. Finally, they are seasoned with a dash of sesame oil.

**Suantou ya** (*swan-toe ya*) 蒜头鸭 Small pieces of duck are first fried and then stir-fried together with copious amounts of garlic and cucumber, then seasoned with chili oil.

**Xingren doufu** (*sing-ren toefoo*) 杏仁豆腐 This dish is called *tofu with almonds*, but in reality it only looks like tofu. It is a sweet pudding with a rather hard consistency, made from condensed milk, rice flour and sugar, aromatized with almond essence, and occasionally garnished with ground pistachio nuts or cherries in syrup.

**Yajia tang** (*ya-jia tang*) 鸭架汤 This is the broth obtained from the carcass of the Beijing crispy duck. It is made with cabbage and tofu and flavored with rice wine and soy sauce. It is usually served after the duck itself.

**Youbao ji** (*yo-bao jee*) 油爆鸡 Diced chicken fried with garlic and cucumber. It is spicy and salty.

**Zui ji** (*dsweh jee*) 醉鸡 Chicken cooked whole in a sauce containing ginger and spring onion, then marinated in rice wine for 48 hours – hence the name *drunken chicken*. It is eaten in tiny pieces on the bone. Served as an appetizer.

# REGIONAL DISHES

The subtropical climate, a sea rich in fish, mollusks and algae, and the perfect environment for duck-rearing and rice cultivation created by the numerous rivers that traverse this region, in addition to a school of unbeatable cooks, have together made Cantonese cuisine the most exquisite and refined in the whole of China. It should come as no surprise then that the most common form of greeting is still *Chifan le ma?* meaning *Have you eaten?* Cooking and eating are part of the art of living; it is no accident that a Chinese proverb runs: "Be born in Suzhou (one of the most beautiful cities in China, the "Venice of the East"), live in Hangzhou (this is where the most beautiful women are to be found), eat in Canton and die in Liuzhou (here they produce a type of wood that is excellent for making coffins)". The high quality of the ingredients on offer makes steaming the preferred cooking method (it preserves the flavor and the natural color of the food). Spices are used only rarely; the natural flavors of the foods are brought out through a skilful interplay of combinations and contrasts.

**Babao daya** (*ba-bao da-ya*) 八宝大鸭 *Duck filled with eight treasures* is a very elaborate dish. The bird is boned and stuffed via the beak with a mixture of glutinous rice, mushrooms, shrimps, lotus seeds, cooked Chinese ham and water chestnuts, which has previously been stir-fried with spring onion and ginger. Following this, the duck is covered in soy sauce and roasted. It is served whole with a cut along the breast to display the *eight treasures*.

# REGIONAL DISHES

**Cha siu** (*cha siu*) 叉烧 In Mandarin this dish is called *chashao* (*cha-shao*). Pork is covered in a thick sauce made from tofu, sweet soya paste, soy sauce, oil, sugar and rice wine, then cooked rapidly in a very hot oven, cut into slices and served on a bed of lettuce. In the oven the sauce turns into a crisp coating that creates a dark ring around each slice.

**Chao jielan** (*chao jie-lan*) 炒芥兰 Stir-fried broccoli or cauliflower, seasoned with mustard seeds.

**Dongjiang yanjiu ji** (*doong-jiang yen-jiu jee*) 东江盐酒鸡 Chicken marinated in soy sauce, rose grappa and five-spice powder (see **Condiments and main ingredients**, p. 29). It is then placed in a deep dish, covered in salt and baked. The salt absorbs the fat, leaving the meat not only dry and crispy but also very flavorsome.

**Guangdong chaofan** (*gwang-doong chao-fan*) 广东炒饭 This is the celebrated *Cantonese stir-fried rice*. Boiled rice is stir-fried together with peas, scrambled egg, diced pork, shrimps and mushrooms. There are numerous variations.

**Heye zhengyu** (*heh-yeh jeng-yoo*) 荷叶蒸渔 This elaborate, tasty dish can be made with either salt water or fresh water fish. In general red mullet, bass, carp or trout is used. The fish is marinated in a sauce made from soy sauce, Hoisin sauce (see **Condiments and main ingredients**, p. 32) and rice wine, then stuffed with a mixture of mushrooms and spring onion. Finally it is wrapped in lotus leaves and either steamed or baked.

**Jiangcong pangxie** (*jiang-tsong pang-sie*) 姜葱螃蟹
Pieces of crab stir-fried with ginger, spring onion, soy sauce, rice wine and sugar.

**Jin zhu** (*jin joo*) 金猪 *Golden piglet.* A suckling pig is covered in a sauce made from garlic, sesame sauce, sugar, sweet bean sauce and rice wine, treated with boiling water and roasted over hot coals for a full day to obtain a crisp golden coating.

**Wucai chaofan** (*woo-tsai chao-fan*) 五彩炒饭 *Stir-fried rice with five colors* is one of the many variations on *Cantonese rice.* This recipe is made using cooked Chinese ham, prawns, mushrooms, peas and scrambled egg, enhanced with fresh onion and finally seasoned with soy sauce.

**Xian heye fan** (*sien heh-yeh fan*) 馅荷叶饭 Lotus leaf parcels filled with glutinous rice and various aromas.

**Xining jipian** (*see-ning jee-pien*) 西拧鸡片 *Chicken with lemon.* This dish appears on Chinese menus the world over: Morsels of chicken are marinated in rice wine and soy sauce, then floured and fried, and seasoned with a sauce made from sugar, lemon, sesame oil and cornstarch. They are served with a garnish of lemon peel cut into thin strips.

# REGIONAL DISHES

## SHANGHAI

Eastern China lies on the vast, fertile plain created by the delta of the Yangtze River, which flows into the sea a few kilometers north of Shanghai. The "classics" of Chinese cuisine come from this region and are made from the typical products of the area: in particular rice and fish (the Chinese eat the eyes), but also soya, a large variety of vegetables and a special type of hairy crab (zhaxie, *ja-sie*), which is cooked with ginger and spring onion. Thanks to its favorable climate this region produces up to three rice harvests a year; rice wine and peanut oil are made here and are widely used throughout the area.

The cuisine of Shanghai is characterized by delicate flavors and the moderate use of spices; food is typically steamed or cooked in lotus leaves, and red sauce (hongyou, *hong-yo*), made from soya, rice wine and sugar, is a common ingredient.

**Basi shuiguo** (*ba-s shweh-gwo*) 拔丝水果  This sweet is much more common abroad than in China itself, where it is eaten predominantly in this area. Pieces of fruit (usually banana or apple) are fried in a light batter and caramelized, and sesame seeds are added.

**Heye fengzheng rou** (*heh-yeh feng-jeng ro*) 荷叶粉蒸肉 These are steamed lotus leaf parcels containing fried pig's entrails and split rice, flavored with garlic, ginger, spring onion, five-spice powder (see **Condiments and main ingredients**, p. 29), sugar and oyster sauce. During cooking the aroma of the lotus leaves impregnates the parcels, giving them a very delicate flavor.

**Jiaoyan xia** (*jiao-yen sia*) 椒盐虾   This unusual, delicate dish is often served as an appetizer. It is made from stir-fried prawns seasoned with minced spring onion and garlic, chili pepper and aniseed. Finally, salt, white pepper and freshly-ground Sichuan pepper are added.

**Juhua rouwan** (*joo-hwa ro-wan*)   菊花肉丸 These are meatballs made from pork, shrimps and mushrooms, flavored with ginger and spring onion, wrapped in strips of omelet and fried rapidly. In Chinese they are called *Chrysanthemum meatballs* because they look like the petals of this flower.

**Nanjing yanshuiya** (*nan-jing yen-shweh-ya*) 南京盐水鸭 This dish is typical of Nanchino. Duck is rubbed with a mixture of salt and roasted Sichuan pepper. It is then steamed and seasoned with a sauce made from light soy sauce, sugar and oil.

**Shanhu baicai** (*shan-hoo bai-tsai*) 珊瑚白菜   Stir-fried Chinese cabbage with shrimps and tofu, seasoned with soy sauce and tomato concentrate and baked. This dish is called *coral cabbage* in Chinese.

**Shizi tou** (*shr-ds toe*) 狮子头 Pork meatballs containing shrimps, bamboo shoots, mushrooms, ginger and spring onion, fried and dipped into a thick sauce made from soya

# REGIONAL DISHES

and chicken broth. The name means *lion's heads* in Chinese.

**Wuxiang paigu** (*woo-siang pai-goo*) 五香排骨 Pork chops marinated in a sauce made from soya, sugar, rice wine, Hoisin sauce and five-spice powder (see **Condiments and main ingredients**, p. 29). They are baked and seasoned with a thickened version of the same sauce and sesame seeds.

**Xiaren guoba** (*sia-ren gwo-ba*) 虾仁锅巴 Prawns marinated in a sauce made from ginger, spring onion and chili pepper, then fried and seasoned with a sauce made from tomato sauce, sugar and vinegar. They are served with *guoba* (see **Gastronomic terms**, p.97), the rice crust that forms at the bottom of the pan during cooking, which is also fried.

**Yangzhou chaofan** (*yang-jo chao-fan*) 扬州 炒饭 Typical dish of the city of Yangzhou. Stir-fried rice with pork, shrimps, scrambled egg, peas, beansprouts, peppers and mushrooms, seasoned with soy sauce and spring onion.

## SICHUAN

The region of Sichuan in southwestern China is vast and extremely fertile, rich in water courses and bamboo forests, where cuddly panda bears roam freely. The area produces large quantities of rice, vegetables, mushrooms and spices; for this reason, and also due to Buddhist influences from nearby Tibet, meat-based dishes are a rarity, while vegetables and tofu are used abundantly, often with chili and spices. In fact in the Sichuan some 20 or so types of pepper and chili pepper are cultivated, including the famous *Sichuan pepper* (huajiao, *hwa-jiao*), a reddish-brown berry that, when roasted and ground, has a pungent aroma considered by some to be like soap. The Chinese also call it *firework*, and it is not hard to imagine why. The most frequently used condiments are sesame oil and the sauce made from the same plant. One specialty of this area is the unusual sauce called *fish-flavored* sauce (yuxiang you, *yoo-siang yo*), made from vinegar, garlic, ginger and soy sauce. Sichuan is also home to a large number of naturally preserved foods (salted, dried, pickled and smoked). This is probably because the particularly humid climate makes conserving fresh foods difficult.

**Chenpi niurou** (*chen-pee niu-ro*) 陈皮牛肉 Thin strips of fried beef seasoned with a sauce made from mandarin peel. Served as an appetizer.

**Dasuan kongxincai** (*da-swan koong-sin-tsai*) 大蒜空心菜 Plant similar to the climbing bellflower, stir-fried with garlic and Sichuan pepper. The name in Chinese means *vegetable with an empty heart* because of its hollow stalk.

**Heye fengzheng niurou** (*heh-yeh feng-jeng niu-ro*) 荷叶粉蒸牛肉 This is a very characteristic dish. Thin slices of beef

are rolled up with a mixture of spiced rice, soy sauce,
Hoisin sauce, ginger, chili pepper and sugar. The slices are
individually bound in lotus leaves and steamed for a few
hours. During cooking the fat from the meat and the other
ingredients combine to form a thick juice that gives the
dish a distinctive aroma.

**Huiguo rou** (*hweh-gwo ro*)  回锅肉  The Chinese name
(*pork that returns to the pan*) implies the fate of the
unfortunate animal: first it is boiled and allowed to cool;
then it is cut into small pieces and stir-fried in a spicy
sauce made from soya, garlic, chili pepper, ginger and
sugar; finally it is sprinkled with spring onion.

**Huoguo** (*hwo-gwo*)  火锅  Many restaurants in Sichuan
display the sign *huoguo* (pan on the heat). The small
tables have a hole at the center and under this there is a
stove that keeps a pan of broth on the boil. Various food
items (meat, vegetables, fish, tofu) are skewered and
cooked rapidly in the broth. This can be fish-based,
chicken-based, or even made from chili pepper. In this
case it can be identified by its bright red color.

**Jinxianyu** (*jin-sien-yoo*) 金线玉 Steamed tofu is diced
and stir-fried together with lean pork, shrimps,
mushrooms, lily flowers, bamboo shoots, ginger and
spring onion.
The dish is then seasoned with soy sauce and sprinkled
with Sichuan pepper. The Chinese think that tofu cooked
in this way is reminiscent of the form and color of

gemstones – hence the name of this dish, which means *jade interwoven with threads of gold.*

**Juju ji** (*joo-joo jee*) 榉榉鸡 Chicken cooked whole in the pan. Once it has cooked it is allowed to cool, then it is cut into strips and seasoned with a sauce made from sesame oil, peanut paste, sugar and broth. It is served as an appetizer, together with slices of cucumber and covered in ground chili pepper.

**Mayi shangshu** (*ma-ee shang-shoo*) 蚂蚁上树 In Chinese this dish is called *ants that climb up the tree.* It is a simple, spicy soup containing minced pork and rice noodles. The strange name derives from the fact that the morsels of meat look like ants walking along the branches of a tree, represented by the noodles.

**Sichuan lazi ji** (*s-chwan la-ds jee*) 四川辣子鸡 Very spicy dish. Small pieces of chicken are stir-fried with ginger and chili pepper and seasoned with soy sauce and rice wine.

**Sichuan qiezi** (*s-chwan chie-ds*) 四川茄子 Fried eggplant seasoned with a sauce made from soya, spring onion, ginger, chili pepper and garlic. It is a very tasty dish and is sometimes served with thin strips of pork.

**Su shijin** (*soo shr-jin*) 素什锦 Stir-fried tofu with vegetables (mushrooms, sweet-peas, bamboo shoots, Chinese cabbage, carrots) and soy sauce, and seasoned with sesame oil.

# REGIONAL DISHES

**Tang yuan** (*tang ywen*) 汤圆  Four sweet ravioli made from rice flour, each with a different filling. The most characteristic version is the one perfumed with osmanthus flowers.

**Xiangsu ya** (*siang-soo ya*) 香酥鸭  Duck covered with Sichuan pepper, cinnamon and aniseed, then basted with rice wine mixed with salt and cooked whole with ginger and spring onion. Following this it is fried (still whole), cut into pieces and served. The individual pieces are dipped into a mixture of salt and Sichuan pepper before eating.

**Youyu guoba** (*yo-yoo gwo-ba*) 鱿渔锅巴  Crisp fried rice (*guoba* is the crust that forms at the bottom of the pan during cooking) served with prawn soup.

**Yuxiang rousi** (*yoo-siang ro-s*) 渔香肉丝  Thin strips of pork are stir-fried with peppers, garlic, spring onion, ginger, egg, mushrooms and bamboo shoots, and seasoned with a sauce made from rice wine, sugar, garlic, soy sauce and cornstarch. The particular sequence in which the ingredients are cooked gives the dish its characteristic and delicate fishy flavor.

**Yuxiang zhugan** (*yoo-siang joo-gan*) 渔香猪干  Pig's liver cut into thin strips and fried rapidly, seasoned with a sauce made from spring onion, ginger, garlic, chili pepper, vinegar and soy sauce. The Chinese call this condiment *fish-flavored sauce*.

**Zhangcha kaoya** (*jang-cha kao-ya*) **樟茶烤鸭** This special dish is eaten on important occasions and is slow and difficult to prepare. Duck is marinated in a mixture of Sichuan pepper, sugar, spring onion, ginger and rice wine for three days, then steamed, aromatized with black tea, Sichuan pepper, brown sugar, cinnamon and aniseed, and finally smoked over camphor wood.

# *RECIPES*

On the whole Chinese recipes are not difficult to make, since mostly fresh ingredients are used; spices and condiments can be obtained from herbalists or organic food shops and in most large towns there are now supermarkets or markets that sell fresh exotic produce such as Chinese cabbage and root ginger. Other, less common ingredients can be substituted without too great a risk to the end result: if you have difficulty getting hold of rice wine you can use dry sherry or balsamic vinegar mixed with a dash of light soy sauce; and Chinese vinegar can be substituted with cider vinegar. Beansprouts are now widely available in supermarkets, but if you have the patience to grow them at home (they need only to be kept in a dark place and watered regularly) you will be rewarded by a delicate, sweet flavor uncommon in the packaged variety. The equipment needed to cook Chinese food can also easily be improvised: instead of a *wok* you can use an iron frying pan (preferably deep), while food can be steamed in a colander placed over a pan of boiling water. The Chinese also make ample use of chopsticks: for adding and removing ingredients from the pan, for mixing, for beating eggs and, as they say, for keeping the food moving. Longer chopsticks are used for this purpose. The following recipes serve four people.

## BASI SHUIGUO
*Deep-fried and caramelized fruit*

### Ingredienti
*2 apples*
*2 bananas*
*1 egg*
*125 g sugar (4$^1/_2$ oz)*
*1 tablespoon sesame seeds*
*4 tablespoons cornstarch*
*3 tablespoons sesame oil*

### Method
Peel the fruit and chop into small pieces. Beat the egg together with the cornstarch and add enough hot water to obtain a fluid batter. Heat the oil in the pan. Dip the fruit into the batter mixture, immerse in the hot oil and deep-fry for 2-3 minutes. Heat the sugar and sesame oil for 5 minutes, add a tablespoon of water and mix well for two minutes. Add the sesame seeds and the fried fruit and stir carefully until it is covered in caramel. At this point remove the fruit and immerse in cold water to harden the caramel.

## Chao shucai
*Stir-fried vegetables*

**Ingredients**

*250 g Chinese cabbage (approx. 9 oz)*
*150 g carrots (approx. $5^1/_2$ oz)*
*150 g broccoli (approx. $5^1/_2$ oz)*
*5-6 dry Chinese mushrooms*
*salt, sugar, light soy sauce*

**Method**

Soak the mushrooms in warm water for 20 minutes and cut into thin strips. Thinly bias-slice the carrots and the cabbage. Separate the heads of broccoli. Heat the oil in the pan, add the cabbage and the carrots and cook for a minute. Add the mushrooms and the broccoli and cook for a further minute. Add the salt and a teaspoon of sugar and mix well. Finally, add a tablespoon of soy sauce and cook for one minute more.

**CHUNJUAN**
*Spring rolls*

### Ingredients

For the pastry:

*225 g flour (8 oz)*
*1 egg*
*salt*

For the filling:

*350 g lean pork, cut into thin strips (approx. 12 $^1/_2$ oz)*
*75 g mushrooms (approx. 2 $^1/_2$ oz)*
*75 g bamboo shoots (approx. 2 $^1/_2$ oz)*
*120 g beansprouts (approx. 4 oz)*
*50 g spring onion (approx. 2 oz)*
*2 thin slices fresh root ginger*
*2 tablespoons soy sauce*
*salt*

### Method

In a mixing bowl, combine the flour, egg, a pinch of salt
and 1 $^1/_2$ glasses of water to obtain a smooth dough, and
leave to rest for 30 minutes. In the meantime, prepare the
filling: heat the oil in the pan and stir-fry the meat for 2-3
minutes; then add the ginger and the vegetables chopped
into thin strips and cook for a further two minutes. Add
the soy sauce and continue to stir-fry for 2 more minutes.
Allow to cool. Shape the dough into a roll about 30 cm

(approx. 2 ½ inches) long and cut into portions measuring approximately 2 fingers in thickness. Flour the slices and roll them out one by one using a rolling-pin to obtain a thin sheet. Cut the pastry sheets into squares measuring 15 x 15 cm (approx. 6 x 6 inches) and arrange on the table top with one of the corners pointing towards you. On the lower half of each square place 2-3 tablespoonfuls of the filling and fold the bottom corner over twice towards the filling. Fold the side corners towards the center and finally close the uppermost corner using a little flour mixed with water to obtain the characteristic rectangular shape. Deep-fry the spring rolls in boiling oil for approximately four minutes and serve immediately.

**Variations**

To make *vegetarian spring rolls*, heat the oil in the pan with a tablespoon of fresh ground ginger. Add 2 carrots chopped into matchstick-sized lengths, 4 green-ribbed leaves and 8 Chinese cabbage leaves cut into thin strips. After 1 minute add 50 g (approx. 2 oz) spring onion, 120 g (approx. 4 oz) beansprouts, 75 g (approx. 2 ½ oz) bamboo shoots, salt and 2 tablespoons of soy sauce. Then follow the instructions in the main recipe.

To make *spring rolls with shrimps*, heat the oil in the pan with 1/2 tablespoon of ground ginger. Add 200 g (7 oz) of peeled shrimps and a pinch of salt. After a minute add 250 g (approx. 9 oz) beansprouts, 50 g (approx. 2 oz) spring onion and 2 tablespoons of soy sauce. Then follow the instructions in the main recipe.

## DANDAN MIAN
*Dandan noodles*

**Ingredients**

*350 g Chinese egg noodles (approx. 12½ oz)*
*200 g minced pork (7 oz)*
*75 g spring onion (approx. 2½ oz)*
*2-3 fresh chili peppers*
*3 cloves garlic*
*a small piece of fresh root ginger (about 2-3 cm)*
*1 tablespoon soy sauce*
*50 g peanuts, crushed (approx. 2 oz)*
*1 teaspoon rice wine*
*2 glasses chicken broth*
*salt*

**Method**

In a bowl, combine the pork, soy sauce, rice wine and a pinch of salt. Heat the oil in the pan, add the meat and brown. Remove the meat using a perforated spoon and set to drain on a sheet of absorbent paper. In the pan, gently fry the garlic, ginger, spring onion and peanuts for 1 minute. Add the broth, bring to the boil and allow the sauce to thicken over a low heat for about 5 minutes. Add the meat and continue to cook for a further minute. Cook the noodles in salted water, strain and season with the sauce together with a generous sprinkling of spring onion and fresh chili pepper.

# RECITES

## GONGBAO JIDING
*Chicken of the deputy king*

### Ingredients
*400 g chicken, diced (approx. 14 oz)*
*150 g bamboo shoots (approx. 5½ oz)*
*50 g spring onion (approx. 2 oz)*
*1 piece fresh root ginger (about 3 cm)*
*50 g peanuts (approx. 2 oz)*
*1 green pepper*
*3-4 fresh red chili peppers*
*1 egg*
*salt*
*1 1/2 tablespoons cornstarch*
*1 clove garlic*
*1 teaspoon sugar*
*2 tablespoons rice wine*

### Method
In a bowl, beat the egg together with a tablespoon of cornstarch, add the chicken and mix well. Heat the oil in the pan and cook the meat for a few minutes. Remove and set to drain on a sheet of absorbent paper. Brown the spring onion together with the ginger, chili pepper, garlic, peanuts, bamboo and finely chopped pepper. Add the chicken, salt, sugar and rice wine and cook for a further minute. Dissolve the remaining cornstarch in a tablespoon of water, pour into the pan and allow to thicken slightly. Serve hot.

## GUANDONG CHAOFAN
*Cantonese stir-fried rice*

### Ingredients
*400 g boiled rice (approx. 14 oz)*
*150 g shrimps, peeled (approx. 5¹/₂ oz)*
*150 g pork or chicken (approx. 5¹/₂ oz)*
*100 g peas, shelled (3¹/₂ oz)*
*salt*
*2 eggs*
*50 g spring onion (approx. 2 oz)*
*1 tablespoon soy sauce*

### Method
Beat the eggs together with a pinch of salt and a tablespoon of finely chopped spring onion. Heat a tablespoon of oil in the pan and add the eggs. Stir continuously until they are cooked and put to one side. In a further 2 tablespoons of oil, stir-fry the shrimps, finely-chopped meat, peas and what is left of the spring onion for 1 minute and season with the soy sauce. Continue to cook for a further 2-3 minutes, then add the rice and the egg, taking care to separate this into small pieces. Cook for 1 minute more, add salt to taste and serve hot.

## GULAO ROU
*Pork in ancient style (sweet and sour pork)*

### Ingredients

*500 g pork (approx. 1 lb)*
*150 g bamboo shoots (approx. 5$\frac{1}{2}$ oz)*
*1 green pepper*
*50 g spring onion (approx. 2 oz)*
*150 g pineapple in syrup (approx. 2 oz)*
*1 egg*
*salt*
*1 tablespoon cornstarch*
*1 tablespoon rice wine*

For the sauce:

*3 tablespoons vinegar*
*3 tablespoons sugar*
*1 tablespoon tomato sauce*
*1 tablespoon soy sauce*
*1 tablespoon cornstarch*
*1 teaspoon sesame oil*

### Method

Dice the meat, place in a bowl together with a pinch of salt and a tablespoon of rice wine and marinate for 15 minutes. Beat the egg, pour into the bowl together with the cornstarch and mix well. Heat the oil in the pan and fry the meat for 3 minutes. Remove the pan from the heat but leave the meat in the pan for a further 2 minutes, then drain and set on a sheet of absorbent paper. Remove the oil, clean the pan, add 2 tablespoons fresh oil and heat. Fry the pepper together with the pineapple and bamboo for 1-2 minutes, stirring continuously. In a bowl, combine all the ingredients for the sauce and pour over the vegetables. Cook for 3 minutes more until the sauce thickens and becomes shiny. Add the pork, stir for 1 minute and serve with a garnish of finely chopped spring onion.

**HONGSHAO YU**
*Praised fish in sweet and sour sauce*

## Ingredients

1 fish (carp, red mullet or bass) of approximately 1 kg
   (approx. 2 lb)
20 g dried mushrooms ($^3/_4$ oz)
50 g bamboo shoots (approx. 2 oz)
3 cloves garlic
50 g spring onion (approx. 2 oz)
3 cm fresh root ginger (approx. 1 inch)
50 g water chestnuts (approx. 2 oz)
salt

For the sweet and sour sauce:

1 tablespoon flour
2 tablespoons soy sauce
2 tablespoons rice wine
1 tablespoon cane sugar
1 tablespoon vinegar
1 tablespoon tomato concentrate
1 tablespoon salt
4 tablespoons broth

## Method

Put the mushrooms to soak in warm water. Clean the fish
and fry whole for 6-8 minutes, turning it over half way
through cooking. Heat the oil in the pan and stir-fry the
mushrooms together with the bamboo, water chestnuts,

garlic, spring onion, ginger and a pinch of salt for 3-4 minutes. Combine all the ingredients for the sauce, pour over the vegetables and allow these to absorb the flavors for a few minutes. Arrange the fish on a serving dish, cover with the condiment and serve immediately.

# RECIPES

 **HUNDUN TANG**
*Wonton soup*

## Ingredients

For the pastry:

*225 g flour (8 oz)*
*1 egg*
*salt*

For the filling:

*150 g pork, minced (approx. 5$^1$/$_2$ oz)*
*150 g shrimps, peeled (approx. 5$^1$/$_2$ oz)*
*50 g spring onion*
*2 tablespoons ground ginger*
*1 teaspoon sugar*
*1 tablespoon rice wine*
*Sichuan pepper*
*salt*

For the broth:

*500 g chicken wings or 1 chicken carcass (approx. 1 lb)*
*50 g fresh root ginger (approx. 2 oz)*
*1 leek*
*2 sticks celery*
*$^1$/$_2$ glass rice wine*
*1 bunch watercress*

## Method

To make the broth (this can be used as the basis for other soups): place the meat in a large saucepan together with the ginger, leek, celery and 2 l water (4 pt). Bring to the boil and cook over a low heat for about two hours, skimming the impurities. Allow to cool and then remove the surface fat. Add the rice wine, bring back to the boil and cook for a further 5 minutes.

Make the pastry as in the recipe for *spring rolls*. To make the filling: in a bowl, combine the meat, spring onion and shrimps; add the sugar, rice wine and a pinch of salt. Take a small ball of the filling mixture and place on a sheet of pastry, in line with one of the corners. Moisten this corner slightly and fold it over the filling; now bring the 2 corners alongside the filling into the center and fix them there. Boil for 2-3 minutes in the broth, add the watercress (without the stems) and a dash of freshly ground Sichuan pepper. Garnish the soup with finely chopped spring onion.

## Variation

To make *fried wonton in sweet and sour sauce*, mix 2 tablespoons sugar together with 3 tablespoons rice wine, 3 tablespoons tomato concentrate, 3 tablespoons orange juice, 1 $1/_2$ tablespoon light soy sauce and 1 tablespoon cornstarch dissolved in 5 tablespoons water. Bring to the boil and simmer for a few minutes. Prepare the *wonton* as above, deep-fry in boiling oil and serve with the hot sauce.

## MAPO DOUFU
*Tofu of the pock-marked old lady*

### Ingredients
*450 g tofu (approx. 16 oz)*
*100 g pork cut into thin strips (3¹/₂ oz)*
*100 g water chestnuts (3¹/₂ oz)*
*75 g spring onion, finely chopped (approx. 2¹/₂ oz)*
*1 tablespoon chili powder*
*2 cloves garlic*
*1 tablespoon cornstarch*
*1 tablespoon sweet bean paste*
*1 tablespoon soy sauce*
*1 tablespoon sesame oil*
*1 teaspoon sugar*
*2¹/₂ glasses chicken broth*
*Sichuan pepper, in granules*
*salt*

### Method
Heat the oil in the pan and cook the meat together with
the chili, garlic and sweet bean paste. Add the broth, soy
sauce and sugar, bring to the boil and add the tofu. Cover
and cook for 1 minute. Dissolve the cornstarch in a drop
of water and add, taking care not to cause the tofu cubes
to disintegrate. As soon as the contents come back to the
boil, remove from the heat, salt and add the remaining
ingredients. Mix well, add the coarsely ground pepper and
serve immediately.

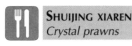

**SHUIJING XIAREN**
*Crystal prawns*

## Ingredients
*350 g prawns (approx. 12¹/₂ oz)*
*1¹/₂ tablespoon cornstarch*
*1 egg white*
*2 tablespoons ground ginger*
*50 g spring onion (approx. 2 oz)*
*100 g peas, half-cooked in salted water (3¹/₂ oz)*
*3 tablespoons vegetable broth*
*1¹/₂ tablespoon rice wine*
*salt*

## Method
Clean the prawns and combine with the egg white,
cornstarch and rice wine; add salt, pepper and a pinch of
sugar. Fry for about 2 minutes and set to drain on a sheet
of absorbent paper. Fry the ginger, spring onion and peas
for 1 minute, then pour in the broth and as soon as the
sauce comes to the boil, add the prawns. Cook for a
further minute and serve.

# RECIPES

 **SICHUAN QIEZI**
*Sichuan-style eggplant*

## Ingredients
*400 g eggplant (approx. 14 oz)*
*50 g spring onion (approx. 2 oz)*
*a small piece of fresh root ginger (about 2-3 cm)*
*1 clove garlic*
*1 tablespoon soy sauce*
*1 teaspoon rice wine*
*1 teaspoon dry, crushed chili pepper*
*2 teaspoons cornstarch*
*salt*

## Method
Peel the eggplant and chop into sticks. Heat the oil in the
pan, add the eggplant and fry for 1-2 minutes. Remove
using a perforated spoon and set to drain on a sheet of
absorbent paper. Remove the oil from the pan, leaving
only a tablespoon. Finely chop the spring onion, ginger
and garlic and stir-fry. Add the soy sauce, rice wine, chili
pepper and eggplant and cook for a further 2-3 minutes.
Dissolve the cornstarch in a drop of water, pour into the
pan and add salt to taste. Allow the contents to thicken
slightly, then remove from the heat and serve immediately.

## SU SHIJIN
*Mixed vegetables with tofu*

### Ingredients
*250 g tofu (approx. 9 oz)*
*5-6 Chinese mushrooms*
*150 g carrots (approx. 5¹/₂ oz)*
*150 g sweet-peas (approx. 5¹/₂ oz)*
*150 g Chinese cabbage (approx. 5¹/₂ oz)*
*150 g bamboo shoots (approx. 5¹/₂ oz)*
*2 fresh onions (approx. 5¹/₂ oz)*
*salt*
*1 tablespoon soy sauce*
*1 tablespoon cornstarch*
*1 teaspoon sugar*
*1 teaspoon sesame oil*

### Method
Dice the tofu and boil for 2-3 minutes. Heat the oil in the pan and add the tofu, stirring repeatedly until it becomes an attractive golden color, then set to drain on a sheet of absorbent paper. Chop the vegetables into small pieces and stir-fry for 2 minutes, then add the tofu and cook for a further minute; add the salt, sugar and soy sauce, lower the heat and cook for 3 more minutes. In the meantime, dissolve the cornstarch in a drop of warm water, pour into the pan and mix, allowing the sauce to thicken. Add the sesame oil and serve immediately.

**SUANLA TANG**
*Spicy and sour soup*

## Ingredients
*1 liter broth (2 pt) – see recipe for wonton soup*
*100 g chicken (3¹/₂ oz)*
*200 g tofu (7 oz)*
*50 g peas (approx. 2 oz)*
*75 g bamboo shoots (approx. 2¹/₂ oz)*
*1 egg*
*2 fresh onions*
*2 tablespoons rice wine*
*1 tablespoon cornstarch*
*2 tablespoons soy sauce*
*1 tablespoon sesame oil*
*salt, pepper and sugar*

## Method
Cut the chicken into thin strips, finely chop the onions
and dice the tofu and the bamboo. Add the ingredients to
the boiling broth. Dissolve the cornstarch in 2 tablespoons
warm water and add this and the condiments, making
sure that there are no lumps. Beat the egg and add to the
soup; wait for it to coagulate slightly and then use
chopsticks to break it up into irregular strands. Remove
from the heat and serve.

**Variations**

Instead of chicken you can use lean pork and add 50 g
(approx. 2 oz) dry Chinese mushrooms, previously put to
soak for 15-20 minutes.

To make a tasty soup with tofu, tomatoes and egg (*Fanqie
danhua tang*, see **National dishes**, p. 51), bring 1 l (2 pt)
chicken broth to the boil, add 2 peeled, de-seeded and
finely chopped tomatoes and 150 g (approx. 5½ oz) diced
tofu and cook for 5 minutes. Beat 2 eggs and pour into the
boiling soup; leave for a moment and then shred (using
chopsticks if possible). After 30 seconds add 50 g (approx.
2 oz) spring onion, a tablespoon of rice wine and a
tablespoon of sesame oil. Add salt and pepper to taste and
serve.

# RECIPES

## WUXIANG PAIGU
*Pork chops with five spices*

**Ingredients**

*1 kg pork chops (approx. 2 lb)*
*3 tablespoons sesame seeds*

For the marinade:

*2 tablespoons soy sauce*
*2 tablespoons rice wine*
*2 tablespoons Hoisin sauce*
*2 tablespoons sugar*
*1 tablespoon dark soy sauce*
*1 teaspoon five-spice powder*
*1 teaspoon salt*

**Method**
Arrange the pork chops in a large dish. Combine the ingredients for the marinade and pour over the meat. Allow to steep for an hour, turning over regularly so that they absorb the condiment. Cook in the oven at 200°C for 40-45 minutes, turning over halfway through cooking. In the meantime, bring the marinade to the boil, adding a dash of water or broth and possibly a tablespoon of cornstarch to thicken it. Pour over the chops and sprinkle with the sesame seeds.

### ZHUACHAO HAIXIAN
*Deep-fried seafood with vegetables*

## Ingredients
*150 g prawns, cleaned (approx. 5¹/₂ oz)*
*4 coquilles St. Jacques*
*1 egg white*
*1 tablespoon cornstarch*
*3 sticks celery*
*1 red pepper*
*2 carrots*
*salt*
*2 cm fresh root ginger (approx. ³/₄ inch)*
*75 g spring onion (approx. 2¹/₂ oz)*
*1 tablespoon rice wine*
*1 tablespoon soy sauce*
*1 teaspoon sesame oil*

## Method
Clean the prawns and the coquilles St. Jacques, chop into
2-3 pieces and place in a bowl together with the egg
white, a pinch of salt and 1/2 tablespoon cornstarch. Heat
the oil in the pan and deep-fry the fish for 1 minute.
Remove and set to drain on a sheet of absorbent paper.
Remove the excess oil from the pan, add the vegetables
and the ginger and cook for about a minute; add the fish,
rice wine, soy sauce and salt. Dissolve the remaining
cornstarch in a drop of water and add to the contents of
the pan. Mix well and season with sesame oil.

# GASTRONOMIC TERMS

**Baijiu** (or **Baigan**) (*bai-jioh* or *bai-gan*)  This is a generic term that refers to liqueurs.

**Basi** (*ba-s*)  Food that is deep-fried and caramelized. The term is usually used to refer to fruit that is dipped in a light batter of flour and water, deep-fried and then immersed in caramelized sugar. Sesame seeds are frequently added.

**Bao** (*bao*)  "Flash" frying: this method involves very rapid frying in very hot oil.

**Bing** (*bing*)  Flat bread, fried or cooked on a griddle.

**Chao** (*chao*)  This term refers to ingredients that are chopped into small, regular pieces and stir-fried in a small amount of very hot oil. It is the most common method of preparing food.

**Chenpi** (*chen-pee*)  Condiment made from mandarin peel. It is usually used to season meat and is typical of the southern regions.

**Chuan** (*chwan*) Small pieces of meat, vegetables or tofu on skewers. They are sold on the street, roasted on the spot and sprinkled with strong, spicy aromas.

**Dianxin** (*dien-sin*)  This generic term is better known in the Cantonese: **dim sum** (*dim sum*). It indicates any kind of small pastry parcel. There are many different types of

# GASTRONOMIC TERMS

dim sum: they come in numerous shapes and with various fillings, and can be either steamed or fried.

**Ding** (*ding*)  Small pieces or cubes. This term refers to one of the basic ways of chopping ingredients.

**Dun** (*doon*)  This means stewed. Food that is cooked slowly in a closed container (usually terracotta) without adding liquid is described in this way.

**Guaiwei** (*gwai-way*)  Sesame sauce. It gives food a spicy, salty, sour and sweet taste all at once. The Chinese call it *sauce with a strange taste.*

**Guoba** (*gwo-ba*)  This is the crust that forms at the bottom of the rice pan during cooking. It is fried and served with soups.

**Hongshao** (*hong-shao*)  This term indicates dishes that are cooked slowly in sauce made from soya, flour, rice wine, sugar and tomato pulp. The sauce gives food a distinctive red color.

**Jian** (*jien*)  This term refers to food that is deep-fried in large quantities of boiling oil.

**Jiucai** (*jioh-tsai*)  Cold appetizers, usually served with rice wine.

**Kao** (*kao*)  This term describes food that is baked.

**Mala** (*ma-la*)  Condiment made from sesame oil, chili pepper, soy sauce and Sichuan pepper.

**Pian** (*pien*)  Thin slices. One method of preparing food, especially meat.

**Shuan** (*shwan*)  This indicates rapid boiling. Food is cut into thin strips and plunged into a pan of broth that is kept on the boil (see **Shuanyangrou**, p. 61 and **Huohuo**, p. 70). This preparation is carried out by the people who are eating.

**Si** (*s*)  Thin strips. One method of chopping food, especially meat.

**Suanla** (*swan-la*)  Spicy and sour. Rice wine, soy sauce and various spices, including pepper and chili pepper, are combined to obtain this flavor.

**Tang** (*tang*) This term indicates soups of varying density.

**Tangcu** (*tang-tsoo*)  Sweet and sour. This is the characteristic flavor that is bitter and sweet at the same time. It is usually obtained by mixing tomato pulp, corn syrup, sugar, pineapple, vinegar and cornstarch.

**Zha** (*ja*)  The classic method of deep-frying in large quantities of boiling oil.

**Zheng** (*jeng*)  This is the method of steaming food in stackable bamboo baskets. Common in the south of

China, steaming maintains the flavor and appearance of food, as well as reducing its fat content.

**Zhou** (*jo*)  This term indicates a porridge-like soup made from cereals that are cooked slowly until they decompose. Rice cooked in this way is eaten by the Chinese for breakfast, and it is frequently used in medicines: it is considered to be the most digestible and nutritious aliment.

**Zhu** (*joo*)  This generic term indicates boiling. The ingredients are immersed in cold water, which is quickly brought to the boil; cooking is then completed over a low heat.

# CONVERSATION 1

## Things to remember

The Chinese always have time for people who can speak even a few words of their language. Many everyday expressions can be said in a variety of ways, all of which are equally common: the more you learn the more likely it is that you will be understood.

My name is...
**Wo jiao...**
*woh jiao...*
我叫...

Thank you
**Xiexie**
*sie-sie*
谢谢

Not at all
**Bu keqi/Bu xie**
*boo ke-chee/boo sie*
不客/气不谢

Excuse me, can I ask...
**Qing wen.../Mafan nin...**
*ching wen.../ma-fan nin...*
请问.../麻烦您...

Sorry (when you run into someone in the street)
**Duibuqi**
*dweh-boo-chee*
对不起

It doesn't matter
**Mei guanxi/mei wenti**
*may gwan-see/may wen-tee*
没关系/没问题

| How do you pronounce this word? | **Zhege zenme nian?** *je-g dsem-moh nien?* 这个怎么念? |
| Can you write it down? | **Ni neng xiexialai ma?** *nee neng sie-sia-lai ma?* 你能写下来吗? |
| Can you speak more slowly, please | **Qing shuo de man yi dian** *ching shwo de man ee-dien* 请说得慢一点 |
| What does it mean? | **Zhe shi shenme yisi?** *je shr shem-moh ee-s?* 这是什么意思? |
| My friend speaks Chinese very well | **Wode pengyou shuo hanyu shuode hen hao** *woh-d peng-yo shwo han-yoo shwo-d hen hao* 我的朋友说汉语说得很好 |
| I need an interpreter | **Wo xuyao yiwei fanyi** *woh soo-yao ee-way fan-ee* 我需要一位翻译 |
| I studied Chinese in Beijing | **Wo zai Beijing xueguo hanyu** *woh dsai bay-jing sweh-gwo han-yoo* 我在北京学过汉语 |

# CONVERSATION 3

| | |
|---|---|
| Where did you study Italian/English? | **Ni zai nar xueguo yidaliyu/yingyu?** *nee dsai nar sweh-gwo ee-da-lee-yoo/ying-yoo?* 你在哪儿学过意大利语/英语? |
| This is my first visit to China | **Zhe shi diyici wo lai Zhongguo** *j shr dee-ee-ts woh lai joong-gwo* 这是第一次我来中国 |
| I will be in Beijing for three days | **Wo yao zai Beijing dai san tian** *woh yao dsai bay-jing dai san tien* 我要在北京呆三天 |
| Pleased to meet you | **Renshi ni wo hen gaoxing** *ren-shr nee woh hen gao-sing* 认识你我很高兴 |
| Today the weather is fine | **Jintian tianqi hen hao** *jin-tien tien-chee hen hao* 今天天气很好 |
| What is the weather forecast for tomorrow? | **Ni zhidao mingtian de tianqi yubao ma?** *nee jr-dao ming-tien d tien-chee yoo-bao ma?* 你知道明天的天气预报吗? |

| | | |
|---|---|---|
| What is today's date? | **Jintian jihao?**<br>*jin-tien jee-hao?*<br>今天几号？ | |
| Today is May 6th, 2000 | **Jintian shi erlinglinglingnian wuyue liuhao**<br>*jin-tien shr ar-ling-ling-ling-nien woo-yweh lioh-hao*<br>今天是二零零零年五月六号 | |
| Monday | **Xingqiyi**<br>*sing-chee-ee* | 星期一 |
| Tuesday | **Xingqier**<br>*sing-chee-ar* | 星期二 |
| Wednesday | **Xingqisan**<br>*sing-chee-san* | 星期三 |
| Thursday | **Xingqisi**<br>*sing-chee-s* | 星期四 |
| Friday | **Xingqiwu**<br>*sing-chee-woo* | 星期五 |
| Saturday | **Xingqiliu**<br>*sing-chee-liu* | 星期六 |
| Sunday | **Xingqitian/Xingqiri**<br>*sing-chee-tien/sing-chee-r* | 星期天<br>星期日 |

| January | **Yiyue** <br> *ee-yweh* | 一月 |
| February | **Eryue** <br> *ar-yweh* | 二月 |
| March | **Sanyue** <br> *san-yweh* | 三月 |
| April | **Siyue** <br> *s-yweh* | 四月 |
| May | **Wuyue** <br> *woo-yweh* | 五月 |
| June | **Liuyue** <br> *lioh-yweh* | 六月 |
| July | **Qiyue** <br> *chee-yweh* | 七月 |
| August | **Bayue** <br> *ba-yweh* | 八月 |
| September | **Jiuyue** <br> *jioh-yweh* | 九月 |
| October | **Shiyue** <br> *shr-yweh* | 十月 |
| November | **Shiyiyue** <br> *shr-ee-yweh* | 十一月 |
| December | **Shieryue** <br> *sh-ar-yweh* | 十二月 |

*Things to remember*

Chopsticks were already in use at the time of the Shang dynasty (16th-11th century BC). The emperor used jade, ivory or silver chopsticks (these were especially useful since they changed color on contact with poison). Chopsticks are not difficult to use but you don't want to be starving when you first try: you will manage to pick up only a small amount of food, at least on the first attempt...

| | |
|---|---|
| I would like to reserve a table for Tuesday evening | **Wo xiang yuding xingqier wanshang de fan**<br>*woh siang yoo-ding sing-chee-ar wan-shang d fan*<br>我想预定星期二晚上的饭 |
| There are four of us | **Si ge ren**<br>*s g ren*<br>四个人 |
| We will arrive at 7.30 p.m. | **Women qidianban lai**<br>*woh-men chee-dien-ban lai*<br>我们七点半来 |
| When do you open/close? | **Ni jidian kaimen/guanmen?**<br>*nee jee-dien kai-men/gwan-men?*<br>你几点开门/关门？ |

| Is there a good restaurant nearby? | **Nar you hao yidian de fanguan?** |
| | *nar yo hao ee-dien d fang-gwan?* |
| | 哪儿有好一点的饭馆？|

| Where can we go to eat Beijing crispy duck? | **Zai nar keyi chidao Beijing kaoya?** |
| | *dsai nar ke-ee chr-dao bay-jing kao-ya?* |
| | 在哪儿可以吃到北京烤鸭？|

| Is it expensive? | **Gui bu gui?** |
| | *gweh boo gweh?* |
| | 贵不贵？|

| How much does it cost per head? | **Meige ren yao hua doushao qian?** |
| | *may-g ren yao hwa doe-shao chien?* |
| | 每个人要花多少钱？|

| We would like to go to a restaurant that serves Sichuanese cuisine | **Women xiang qu yijia Sichuan fandian** |
| | *woh-men siang choo ee-jia s-chwan fan-dien* |
| | 我们想去一家四川饭馆 |

| | |
|---|---|
| Do you have a table? | **You kong weizi ma?** <br> *yo koong way-ds ma?* <br> 有空位子吗？ |
| Is there a menu in English? | **You yingwen de caidan ma?** <br> *yo ying-wen de tsai-dan ma?* <br> 有英文的菜单吗？ |
| What is the house specialty? | **Nimen de teshu fengwei cai shi shenme?** <br> *nee-men d te-shoo feng-way tsai shr shem-moh?* <br> 你们的特殊风味菜是什么？ |
| What dish do you recommend? | **Ni neng tuijian yixie cai ma?** <br> *nee neng tweh-jien ee-sie tsai ma?* <br> 你能推荐一些菜吗？ |
| Could we move to a different table? | **Neng huan ge zhuozi ma?** <br> *neng hwan g jwo-ds ma?* <br> 能换个桌子吗？ |
| What do you have in the way of drinks? | **Nimen you shenme yinliao?** <br> *nee-men yo shem-moh yin-liao?* <br> 你们有什么饮料？ |
| Two bottles of beer, please | **Qing lai liang ping pijiu** <br> *ching lai liang ping pee-jioh* <br> 请来凉瓶啤酒 |

| Do you have any ice-cold Coca-Cola? | **You mei you bingzhen Kekou Kele?** |
| | *yo may yo bing-jen ke-ko ke-le?* |
| | 有没有冰镇可口可乐？ |

| Can we order? | **Keyi diancai le ma?** |
| | *ke-ee dien-tsai l ma?* |
| | 可以点菜了吗？ |

| I'd like stir-fried rice with vegetables | **Wo xiang chi shucai chaofan** |
| | *woh siang chr shoo-tsai chao-fan* |
| | 我想吃蔬菜炒饭 |

| What do you have in the way of soups? | **Nimen you shenme tang?** |
| | *nee-men yo shem-moh tang?* |
| | 你们有什么汤？ |

| I don't like hot food | **Wo bu ai chi lade dongxi** |
| | *woh boo ai chr la-d dong-see* |
| | 我不爱吃辣的东西 |

| I am vegetarian. I eat eggs, tofu and dairy products | **Wo chi su. Wo chi jidan, doufu he naizhipin** |
| | *woh chr soo. woh chr jee-dan, toefoo heh nai-jr-pin* |
| | 我吃素．我吃鸡蛋，豆腐和 奶制品 |

| | |
|---|---|
| What duck dishes do you have? | **Nimen you shenme ya zuode cai?**<br>*nee-men yo shem-moh ya dswo-d tsai?*<br>你们有什么鸭作的菜？ |
| What kind of meat is it? | **Zhe shi shenme rou?**<br>*j shr shem-m ro?*<br>这是什么肉？ |
| Please don't use too much chili pepper | **Bu yao tai lade**<br>*boo yao tai la-d*<br>不要太辣的 |
| I don't know how to use chopsticks | **Wo bu hui yong kuaizi**<br>*woh boo hweh yong kwai-ds*<br>我不会用筷子 |
| Please could you bring me a fork | **Qing gei wo yige chazi**<br>*ching gay woh ee-g cha-ds*<br>清给我一个叉子 |
| Could you show me how to eat with chopsticks? | **Ni jiaojiao wo yong kuaizi, hao ma?**<br>*nee jiao-jiao woh yong kwai-ds, hao ma?*<br>你教教我用筷子好吗？ |
| It is cold | **Cai liang le**<br>*tsai liang l*<br>菜凉了 |

I am allergic
to seafood

**Wo chi haixian hui guomin**
*woh chr hai-sien hweh gwo-min*
我吃海鲜会过敏

Is there any
soy sauce?

**You jiangyou ma?**
*yo jiang-yo ma?*
有酱油吗？

Could you write
down the name
of this dish, please?

**Ni neng bang wo xie xia
caiming ma?**
*nee neng bang woh sie sia
tsai-ming ma?*
你能帮我写下菜名吗？

Very good

**Hen haochi**
*hen hao-chr*
很好吃

The bill, please

**Jiezhang ba**
*jie-jang ba*
结账吧

*Things to remember*

In 1790, to mark the 80th birthday of the Emperor Qianlong, a rural theatre company performed in the capital, engendering the famous Beijing Opera. The genre grew to fame in the West thanks to the actor Mei Lanfang (1894-1961), who was particularly adept at playing *dan*, or female roles.

| | |
|---|---|
| I'd like to see a show | **Wo xiang kan jiemu** <br> *woh siang kan jie-moo* <br> 我想看节目 |
| I'm interested in the Beijing Opera | **Wo dui jingju hen gan xingqu** <br> *woh dweh jing-joo hen gan sing-choo* <br> 我对京剧很感兴趣 |
| What is on at the theatre today? | **Jintian juyuan yan shenme?** <br> *jin-tien joo-yuen yen shen-moh?* <br> 今天剧院演什么？ |
| How much are tickets? | **Mai piao duoshao qian?** <br> *mai piao dwo-shao chien?* <br> 买票多少钱？ |
| Two tickets for seats in the front row | **Wo yao mai liang zhang qianpai de piao** <br> *woh yao mai liang jang chien-pai d piao* <br> 我要买两张前排的票 |

| Where can I get hold of a program? | **Zai nar you jiemudan?** |
| | *dsai nar yo jie-moo-dan?* |
| | 在那儿有节目单？ |

| What time does the show end? | **Jiemu shenme shihou jieshu?** |
| | *jie-moo shen-m shr-ho jie-shoo?* |
| | 节目什么时候结束？ |

| What film is showing today? | **Jintian yan shenme dianying?** |
| | *jin-tien yen shen-m dien-ying?* |
| | 今天演什么电影？ |

| Is it in Italian/ English? | **Shi Yidaliwen/Yingwen duibai ma?** |
| | *shr ee-da-lee-wen/ying-wen dweh-bai ma?* |
| | 是意大利文／英文对白吗？ |

| Are there English subtitles? | **You Yingwen zimu ma?** |
| | *yo ying-wen ds-moo ma?* |
| | 有英文字幕吗？ |

| Who directed this film? | **Zhege yingpian de daoyan shi shei?** |
| | *je-g ying-pien d dao-yen shr shay?* |
| | 这个影片的导演是谁？ |

| When was it made? | **Zhebu yingpian shi nainian de shangyingde?** |
| | *je-boo ying-pien shr nai-nien d shang-ying-d?* |
| | 这部影片是哪年的上映的？ |

# GOURMET SHOPPING 1

*Things to remember*

The most interesting places to make food purchases in China are undoubtedly the so-called "free markets" (ziyou shichang): these can be huge, and sell spices, mushrooms, roots, vegetables and animals of all kinds. Fresh, dried, live, tinned or in small pieces: the food shopper is spoiled for choice.

| | |
|---|---|
| Is there a market near here? | **Fujin you ziyou shichang ma?** *foo-jin yo ds-yo shr-chang ma?* 附近有自由市场吗？ |
| Can you help me? | **Qing bang yixia mang** *ching bang ee-sia mang* 请帮一下忙 |
| Could you show me that, please | **Qing gei wo nage kankan** *ching gay woh ne-g kan-kan* 请给我那个看看 |
| How much does it cost? | **Duoshao qian?** *dwo-shao chien?* 多少钱？ |
| It's too expensive | **Tai guile** *tai gweh-l* 太贵了 |

| How much does it cost per kilo? | **Yi gongjin duoshao qian?** |
| | *ee goong-jin dwo-shao chien?* |
| | 一公斤多少钱？ |

| Is it fresh? | **Xinxian ma?** |
| | *sin-sien ma?* |
| | 新鲜吗？ |

| Give me half a kilo | **Qing gei wo yi jin** |
| | *ching gay woh ee jin* |
| | 请给我一斤 |

| How long does it keep? | **Guoqi shi nayitian?** |
| | *gwo-chee shr na-ee-tien?* |
| | 过期是哪一天？ |

| Two bottles of rose brandy | **Liang ping meiguilu** |
| | *liang ping may-gweh-loo* |
| | 两瓶玫瑰露 |

| Can you give me a discount? | **Neng pianyi dian ma?** |
| | *neng pien-ee dien ma?* |
| | 能便宜点吗？ |

| | |
|---|---|
| Hello | **Ni hao**<br>*nee hao*<br>你好 |
| Good morning | **Nin zao/zaochen hao**<br>*nin dsao/dsao-chen hao*<br>您早/ 早晨好 |
| Good evening | **Wanshang hao**<br>*wan-shang hao*<br>晚上好 |
| Good night | **Wan'an**<br>*wan'an*<br>晚安 |
| Goodbye | **Zaijian**<br>*dsai-jien*<br>再见 |
| See you<br>tomorrow | **Mingtian zaijian**<br>*ming-tien dsai-jien*<br>明天再见 |
| How are you? | **Ni hao ma?**<br>*nee hao ma?*<br>你好吗？ |
| Fine, thank you.<br>And you? | **Wo hen hao, xiexie. Ni ne?**<br>*woh hen hao, sie-sie. nee n?*<br>我很好，谢谢. 你呢？ |

*Things to remember*

> Alongside the Western calendar, the lunar calendar is still in use in China, and it continues to determine various moments in the agricultural cycle, as well as traditional Chinese holidays. Civil holidays have their roots in the "modern", or rather post-imperial, era in China.

| | |
|---|---|
| January 1st | New Year's Day |
| March 8th | Women's Day (holiday for women) |
| May 1st | Labor Day |
| May 4th | Commemoration of the student demonstrations of May 4th, 1919 |
| June 1st | Children's Day (holiday for children) |
| July 1st | Anniversary of the foundation of the Chinese Communist Party |
| August 1st | Feast of the People's Liberation Army |
| October 1st | Anniversary of the foundation of the People's Republic of China |

Spring festival     春节     the 1ˢᵗ day of the 1ˢᵗ month
**Chun jie** (*choon jie*)

*This is the most important festival of the year, when the Chinese celebrate the beginning of spring. On this occasion, the Chinese hang the so-called "spring couplets" (phrases that bring good luck) on the front door; they also let off firecrackers (in ancient times they used to burn bamboo canes; being hollow, these would explode when the air inside them heated up), and eat jiaozi (see* **Dim sum***, p. 39).*

Mid-autumn festival     中秋节     15ᵗʰ day of the 8ᵗʰ month
**Zhongqiu jie** (*joong-choo jie*)

*Falling exactly half way through the autumn, this is the festival of the family: families gather to contemplate the full moon and eat moon biscuits (see* **yuebing***, p. 41).*

Dragon-boat festival     端午节     5ᵗʰ day of the 5ᵗʰ month
**Duanwu jie** (*dwan-woo jie*)

*This festival marks the death of the poet Qu Yuan, a nobleman who held a high position in the court of the kingdom of Chu at the time of the Warring States. He was slandered by his enemies and subsequently exiled; overcome by grief at his failure to impose his political ideas and disgusted by the lack of understanding on the part of the people whom he considered his friends, he drowned himself in the Miluo river. During this festival, dragon-shaped boats take part in regattas and* zongzi *(see* **Dim sum***) are thrown into the river.*

Lantern festival 元宵节 15th day of the 1st month
**Yuanxiao jie** *(ywen-siao jie)*

*On this night, the Chinese customarily light lanterns and go outside to contemplate the full moon.*

Festival of the double nine 重阳节 9th day of the 9th month
**Chongyang jie** *(choong-yang jie)*

*In ancient times the number nine was thought to be a* yang *number, the symbol of wealth and happiness; and so this day is considered particularly lucky. The Chinese traditionally mark the occasion by climbing onto high ground and admiring the chrysanthemums in flower.*

*Things to remember*

In China, large hotels belonging to international chains such as Holiday Inn, Hyatt, Sheraton, etc. now abound. These are equipped with a full range of services. However, English-speaking staff are still few and far between…

| | |
|---|---|
| I've reserved a room for two nights | **Wo yuding le yige fangjian zhu liangge wanshang**<br>*woh yoo-ding l ee-g fang-jien joo liang-g wan-shang*<br>我预定了一个房间住两个晚上 |
| Do you have a single/ double room? | **You danren/shuangren fangjian ma?**<br>*yo dan-ren/shwang-ren fang-jien ma?*<br>有单人/双人房间吗？ |
| How much is it per day? | **Meitian duoshao qian?**<br>*may-tien dwo-shao chien?*<br>每天多少钱？ |
| Is breakfast included in the price? | **Jiaqian li baokuo zaofan ma?**<br>*jia-chien lee bao-kwo dsao-fan ma?*<br>价钱里包括早饭吗？ |
| Is there a discount for foreign students? | **Dui liuxuesheng you mei you youhui?**<br>*dweh liu-sweh-sheng yo may yo yo hweh?*<br>对留学生有没有优惠？ |

| | |
|---|---|
| We're staying for one night/three nights/a week | **Women xiang zhu yi tian/ san tian/yige xingqi** <br> *woh-men siang joo ee tien/ san tien/ee-g sing-chee* <br> 我们想住一天／ 三天／一个星期 |
| We would like two rooms close together | **Women yao liangge jin'aizhe de fangjian** <br> *woh-men yao liang-g jin-ai-j de fang-jien* <br> 我们要两个紧挨着的房间 |
| Could you carry my luggage to my room, please It's no. 345 | **Qing ba xingli songdao wo de fangjian. Fangjian haoma shi sansiwu** <br> *ching ba sing-lee soong-dao woh de fang-jien. fang-jien hao-ma shr san-s-woo* <br> 请把行李送到我的房间. 房间号码是三四五 |
| Where should I leave my key? | **Wo yinggai ba yaoshi fang zai nar?** <br> *woh ying-gai ba yao-shr fang dsai nar?* <br> 我应该把钥匙放在哪儿? |

| | |
|---|---|
| Please could I be woken at 7.30? | **Qing zai mingtian qidianban jiao xing wo**<br>*ching dsai ming-tien chee-dien-ban jiao sing woh*<br>请在明天七点半叫醒我 |
| What time is breakfast/ lunch/dinner? | **Shenme shijian kai zaofan/wufan/wanfan?**<br>*shen-moh shr-jien kai dsao-fan/woo-fan/wan-fan*<br>什么时间开早饭/午饭/晚饭？ |
| Could I have another blanket/pillow? | **Neng zai gei wo yitiao tanzi/zhentou ma?**<br>*neng dsai gay woh ee-tiao tan-ds/jen-toe ma?*<br>能再给我一条毯子/枕头吗？ |
| Please could you bring me a thermos of boiled water | **Qing na yi ping kaishui lai**<br>*ching na ee-ping kai-shweh lai*<br>请拿一瓶开水来 |
| How do you turn off the air conditioning? | **Kongtiao zenme guan?**<br>*koong-tiao dsem-moh gwan?*<br>空调怎么关？ |
| There is no hot water | **Meiyou reshui**<br>*may-yo r-shweh*<br>没有热水 |

*Things to remember*

> Admission to places of interest is normally twice as much for foreigners as it is for the Chinese. It is also usual to have to buy more than one ticket to explore the different parts of a building or garden: no-one is trying to get the better of you.

| | |
|---|---|
| I'd like a map of this place | **Qing gei wo yi zhang bendi ditu**<br>*ching gay woh ee jang ben-dee dee-too*<br>清给我一张本地地图 |
| I'd like to go to the Pagoda of the Big Wild Goose | **Wo xiang qu Dayan Ta**<br>*woh siang choo ta-yen ta*<br>我想去大雁塔 |
| Is it possible to walk there? | **Zou de dao ma?**<br>*dso d dao ma?*<br>走得到吗? |
| What bus must I take to get to the Summer Palace? | **Qu Yiheyuan zuo na lu che?**<br>*choo ee-heh-yuen dswo na loo che?*<br>去颐和园坐哪路车? |
| Where is the nearest bus stop? | **Zuijin de gonggong qiche zhan zai nar?**<br>*dsweh-jin d goong-goong chee-che jan dsai nar?*<br>最近的公共汽车站在哪儿? |

A ticket for
Wangfujing

**Yi zhang Wangfujing**
*ee jang wang-foo-jing*
一张王府井

How many stops
is it to Tiananmen
Square?

**Qu Tiananmen Guangchang you ji zhan?**
*choo tien-an-men gwang-chang yo jee jan?*
去天安门广场有几站？

Could you tell me
when we get there,
please?

**Dao zhan qing jiao wo yixia**
*dao jan ching jiao woh ee-sia*
到站请叫我一下

Is this Chang'an
Street?

**Zhe shi Chang'an dajie ma?**
*je shr chang-an da-jie ma?*
这是长安大街吗？

How long does
it take to get
to Liulichang?

**Dao Liulichang you duo yuan?**
*dao lioh-lee-chang yo dwo yuen?*
到琉璃厂有多远？

Can you tell me
the way?

**Ni neng gaosu wo zenme qu ma?**
*nee neng gao-soo woh dsem-moh choo ma?*
你能告诉我怎么去吗？

Where can I find a
public toilet?

**Gongyong cesuo zai nar?**
*goong-yong ts-swo dsai nar?*
公用厕所在哪儿？

# MONEY 1

*Things to remember*

> In China the exchange rate for foreigners, FEC (Foreign Certificate Exchange), was operational until 1994. Nowadays it is possible to change most major currencies in large hotels, while at the bank dollars are preferred. Banking operations are most easily carried out at the Bank of China, which is the national bank.

Is there a bank in the vicinity?

**Fujin you mei you yinhang?**
*Foo-jin yo may yo yin-hang?*
附近有没有银行？

I would like to change some US dollars

**Wo yao duihuan Yidali lila**
*woh yao dweh-hwan may-ywen*
我要兑换意大利里拉

I have traveler's checks

**Wo you luxing zhipiao**
*woh yo loo-sing jr-piao*
我有旅行支票

Do you take credit cards?

**Neng yong xinyongka?**
*neng yong sin-yong-ka?*
能用信用卡？

Could you give me bills in small denominations, please

**Qing gei wo xiao piaozi**
*ching gay woh siao piao-ds*
请给我小票子

| | |
|---|---|
| What is the exchange rate? | **Duihuan lu shi duoshao?** <br> *dweh-hwan loo shr dwo-shao?* <br> 兑换率是多少? |
| Do you charge commission? | **You mei you fuwu fei?** <br> *yo may yo foo-woo fay?* <br> 有没有服务费? |
| May I have a receipt? | **Neng gei wo yi zhang fapiao ma?** <br> *neng gay woh ee jang fa-piao ma?* <br> 能给我一张发票吗? |
| Do you accept dollars? | **Nimen shou mei yuan ma?** <br> *nee-men sho may ywen ma?* <br> 你们受美元吗? |
| Can I draw cash with my credit card? | **Keyi yong xinyongka qu qian ma?** <br> *ke-ee yong sin-yong-ka choo chien ma?* <br> 可以用信用卡取钱吗? |
| Is it possible to cash this traveler's check? | **Nimen shou zhe zhang luxing zhipiao ma?** <br> *nee-men sho je jang loo-sing jr-piao ma?* <br> 你们受这张旅行支票吗? |

# MONEY 3

## Things to remember

> The currency in China is the Renminbi ("the currency
> of the people"). Its principal unit is the yuan, which is
> divided into ten jiao, each of which is in turn divided
> into ten fen. In spoken Chinese, the word kuai is
> frequently used instead of yuan and mao instead of
> jiao. The last word that defines the figure is left out.
> Today fen are rarely used.

| | | |
|---|---|---|
| Y 15 | **shiwu kaui** | *shr-woo kwai* |
| Y 15.65 | **shiwu kuai liu mao wu** | *shr-woo kwai liu mao woo* |
| Y 1.50 | **yi kuai wu** | *ee kwai woo* |
| Y 0.30 | **san mao** | *san mao* |
| Y 0.32 | **san mao er** | *san mao ar* |
| Y 0.20 | **liang fen** | *liang fen* |

## Foreign currencies

| | | |
|---|---|---|
| Italian lire | **Yidali lila**<br>*ee-da-lee lee-la* | 意大利里拉 |
| US dollars | **Meiyuan**<br>*may-ywen* | 美元 |
| British sterling | **Yingbang**<br>*ying-bang* | 英镑 |
| French francs | **Faguo falang**<br>*fa-gwo fa-lang* | 法国法郎 |
| German marks | **Deyizhi make**<br>*de-ee-jr ma-k* | 德意志马克 |
| Japonese yen | **Riyuan**<br>*r-ywen* | 日元 |
| Hong Kong dollars | **Gangbi**<br>*gang-bee* | 港币 |
| Australian dollars | **Aoyuan**<br>*ao-ywen* | 澳元 |

# NUMBERS 1

| | | |
|---|---|---|
| 0 ling 零<br>*ling* | 11 shiyi 十一<br>*shr-ee* | 40 sishi 四十<br>*s-shr* |
| 1 yi 一<br>*ee* | 12 shier 十二<br>*shr-ar* | 50 wushi 五十<br>*woo-shr* |
| 2 er 二<br>*ar* | 13 shisan 十三<br>*shr-san* | 60 liushi 六十<br>*liu-shr* |
| 3 san 三<br>*san* | 14 shisi 十四<br>*shr-s* | 70 qishi 七十<br>*chee-shr* |
| 4 si 四<br>*s* | 15 shiwu 十五<br>*shr-woo* | 80 bashi 八十<br>*ba-shr* |
| 5 wu 五<br>*woo* | 16 shiliu 十六<br>*shr-liu* | 90 liushi 九十<br>*jioh-shr* |
| 6 liu 六<br>*liu* | 17 shiqi 十七<br>*shr-chee* | 100 yibai 一百<br>*ee-bai* |
| 7 qi 七<br>*chee* | 18 shiba 十八<br>*shr-ba* | 200 erbai 二百<br>*ar-bai* |
| 8 ba 八<br>*ba* | 19 shijiu 十九<br>*shr-jioh* | 300 sanbai 三百<br>*san-bai* |
| 9 jiu 九<br>*jioh* | 20 ershi 二十<br>*ar-shr* | 400 sibai 四百<br>*s-bai* |
| 10 shi 十<br>*shr* | 30 sanshi 三十<br>*san-shr* | 500 wubai 五百<br>*woo-bai* |

# NUMBERS 2

| | | | | | | |
|---|---|---|---|---|---|---|

600 **liubai** 六百
*lioh-bai*

700 **qibai** 七百
*chee-bai*

800 **babai** 八百
*ba-bai*

900 **jiubai** 九百
*jioh-bai*

1.000 一千
**yiqian** (*ee-cien*)

10.000 一万
**yiwan** (*ee-wan*)

100.000 一百万
**yibaiwan** (*ee-bai-wan*)

1.000.000 一千万
**yiqianwan** (*ee-chien-wan*)

1st **diyi** 第一
*dee-ee*

2nd **dier** 第二
*dee-ar*

3rd **disan** 第三
*dee-san*

4th **disi** 第四
*dee-s*

5th **diwu** 第五
*dee-woo*

6th **diliu** 第六
*dee-lioh*

7th **diqi** 第七
*dee-chee*

8th **diba** 第八
*dee-ba*

9th **dijiu** 第九
*dee-jioh*

10th **dishi** 第十
*dee-shr*

# PAYING

*Things to remember*

> Credit cards and traveler's checks are accepted in
> large hotels and major tourist stores only. For
> everything else (including airplane and train tickets),
> you must pay in cash.

| | |
|---|---|
| The bill, please | **Jiezhang ba** <br> *jie-jang ba* <br> 结账吧 |
| Can I pay by credit card? | **Neng yong xinyongka?** <br> *neng yoong sin-yoong-ka?* <br> 能用信用卡？ |
| Do you accept traveler's checks? | **Neng yong luxing zhipiao?** <br> *neng yoong loo-sing jr-piao?* <br> 能用旅行支票？ |
| How much is it? | **Duoshao qian?** <br> *dwo-shao chien?* <br> 多少钱？ |
| Could I have a receipt? | **Neng gei wo yi zhang fapiao ma?** <br> *neng gay woh ee jang fa-piao ma?* <br> 能给我一张发票吗？ |
| Can you give me a discount? | **Neng pianyi dian ma?** <br> *neng pien-ee dien ma?* <br> 能便宜点吗？ |

# *PRONUNCIATION*

The system of transcribing Chinese characters, Pinyin, is based on the rules of pronunciation of Russian and German. It is very accurate and solves the various problems of transcribing a language that is phonetically very different from our own. However, unfortunately it is somewhat complicated and, unless we know it well, we risk pronouncing the Chinese words in such a way that they are incomprehensible to our interlocutor. Therefore, in this handbook the transcription in Pinyin is accompanied by a simplified translitteration, which, being pronounced as it is written, is less accurate but more easily leggible than the Pinyin. However, it is worth taking note of a few brief observations:

The syllables are pronounced separately and are all accented.

**h** is aspirated
**r** has a slightly rounded sound, as in the word "try"
syllables represented by a single letter (d, e, g, j, l, m, n, s) are pronounced phonetically. So, the syllable **d** is pronounced as in the word "dog", **g** as in "get", **j** as in "jet", **l** as in "let", etc.

# SIGNALS 1

| | |
|---|---|
| Way in | 入口 |
| Way out | 出口 |
| Gentleman | 男厕所 |
| Ladies | 女厕所 |
| No entry | 禁止入内 |
| No smoking | 禁止吸烟 |
| One way | 单街道 |

| | |
|---|---|
| **Town center** | 市中心 |
| **Police** | 警察 |
| **Open** | 开门 |
| **Closed** | 关门 |
| **Public telephone** | 公用电话 |
| **Checkout** | 收款台 |
| **Water not suitable for drinking** | 非饮用水 |

## Things to remember

> Taxis are easy to come by and are reasonably cheap, but fares vary from one city to another and according to the kind of car. To explain to the driver where you want to go, simply show him the name of your destination written in Chinese on a slip of paper.

| | |
|---|---|
| Where can I get a taxi? | **Nar neng jiaodao chuzu qiche?** <br> *nar neng jiao-dao choo-dsoo chee-che?* <br> 哪儿能叫到出租汽车？ |
| I would like to go to the Sky Temple | **Wo xiang qu Tiantan** <br> *woh siang choo tien-tan* <br> 我想去天坛 |
| What is the rate per kilometer? | **Yi gongli duoshao qian?** <br> *ee goong-lee dwo-shao chien?* <br> 一公里多少钱？ |
| Can you take me to this address, please? | **Ni neng ba wo songdao zhege difan?** <br> *Nee neng ba woh soong-dao je-g dee-fan?* <br> 你能把我送到这个地方？ |
| To Hotel Beijing, please | **Qing kai dao Beijing Fandian** <br> *ching kai dao bay-jing fan-dien* <br> 请开到北京饭店 |
| Please stop here | **Qing ting yixia** <br> *ching ting ee-sia* <br> 请停一下 |

*Things to remember*

> One of the many legends concerning the origins of tea relates that Buddha vowed to stay awake for seven consecutive years; after five years, overcome by a sudden drowsiness, he pulled out his eyelashes and threw them on the ground, so conceiving the tea plant and managing to fulfill his vow.

I'd like a cup of black tea

**Wo xiang he yiwan hongcha**
*woh siang heh ee-wan hong-cha*
我相喝一碗红茶

How much is jasmine tea?

**Huacha duoshao qian?**
*hwa-cha dwo-shao chien?*
花茶多少钱？

What kind of tea is this?

**Zhe shi shenme cha?**
*j shr shem-moh cha?*
这是什么茶？

I would like to see that teapot, please

**Qing gei wo nage chahu kankan**
*ching gay woh ne-g cha-hoo kan-kan*
请给我那个茶壶看看

This tea is cold

**Cha liang le**
*cha liang-l*
茶凉了

*Things to remember*

International calls can be made from hotel telephones
or public callboxes without any difficulty. Telephone
cards are available from hotels, post offices and
department stores. There are "national" cards (quanguo
guojia), which can be used throughout China and cost
100 and 200 yuan, and "regional" cards (bendide),
which function only in the province in which they are
purchased, and cost 50, 100 and 200 yuan. You will
often find a telephone in small stores, but these are not
suitable for making international calls.

| | |
|---|---|
| Is there a telephone nearby? | **Fujin you dianhua ma?**<br>*foo-jin yo dien-hwa ma?*<br>附近有电话吗？ |
| I would like to make a telephone call to the United States | **Wo xiang gei Meiguo da yi ge changtu dianhua**<br>*woh siang gay may-gwo da ee g chang-too dien-hwa*<br>我想给意大利打一个长途电话 |
| The number is 4287358 | **Haoma shi si er ba qi san wu ba**<br>*hao-ma shr s ar ba chee san woo ba*<br>号码是四二八七三五八 |
| What is the per minute rate to New York? | **Gei Niuyue da changtu yi fenzhong duoshao qian?**<br>*gay niu-yweh da chang-too ee fen-joong dwo-shao chien?*<br>给罗马打长途一分钟多少钱？ |

It's a reverse
charge call

**Duifang fukuan**
*dweh-fang foo-kwan*
对方付款

I'm paying
for the call

**Wo fukuan**
*woh foo-kwan*
我付款

I am paying
by credit card

**Wo yong xinyongka fukuan**
*woh yong sin-yong-ka foo-kwan*
我用信用卡付款

The line is bad

**Xianlu bu qingchu**
*sien-loo boo ching-choo*
线路不清楚

The number
is incorrect

**Haoma cuo le**
*hao-ma tswo l*
号码错了

| | |
|---|---|
| What time is it? | **Xianzai jidian?**<br>*sien-dsai jee-dien?*<br>现在几点？ |
| It is... | **Xianzai shi...**<br>*sien-dsai shr...*<br>现在是… |
| 8.00 | **Badian/badian zhong**<br>*ba-dien/ba-dien joong*<br>八点/八点种 |
| 8.15 | **Badian yike/badian shiwu fen**<br>*ba-dien ee-ke/ba-dien shr-woo fen*<br>八点一刻/八点十五分 |
| 8.30 | **Badian ban/badian sanshi fen**<br>*ba-dien ban/ba-dien san-shr fen*<br>八点半/八点三十分 |
| 8.45 | **Badian sanke/badian sishiwu fen**<br>*ba-dien san-ke/ba-dien s-shr-woo fen*<br>八点三刻/八点四十五分 |
| Midday/midnight | **Zhongwu/Banye**<br>*joong-woo/ban-yeh*<br>中午/半夜 |

*Things to remember*

Nowadays, unlike in the past, tipping is a common practice in China, and everyone who comes into contact with tourists – guides, drivers, porters – expects to receive something. There is no set rate as such; the best thing is to use your common sense and leave a tip only if you are satisfied with the service.

| | |
|---|---|
| Is it necessary to leave a tip? | **Yinggai xiaofei ma?**<br>*ying-gai siao-fay ma?*<br>应该小费吗？ |
| Is the tip included? | **Xiaofei baokuole ma?**<br>*siao-fay bao-kwo-l ma?*<br>小费包括了吗？ |
| Keep the change | **Ni ba fubi ba**<br>*nee ba foo-bee ba*<br>你把辅币巴 |
| I don't have any small change | **Wo meiyou lingqian**<br>*woh may-yo ling-chien*<br>我没有零钱 |
| Can you change 10 yuan for 1 yuan bills? | **Qing ni huan yizhang shiyuan gen shizhang yiyuan**<br>*ching nee hwan ee-jang shr-yuen gen shr-jang ee-yuen*<br>请你换一张十元根十张一元 |

# TOILETTE

## Things to remember

Hotels and restaurants of a certain calibre have western-style toilets and are no cause for concern. Public toilets, on the other hand (and there is one on every street corner), are definitely to be avoided because of the poor hygiene and lack of privacy.

Where is the toilet? **Cesuo zai nar?**
*ts-swo dsai nar?*
厕所在哪儿？

Do I have to pay? **Yinggai fukuan ma?**
*ying-gai foo-kwan ma?*
应该付款吗？

There isn't any soap/toilet paper **Meiyou xiangzao/weisheng zhi**
*may-yo siang-dsao/way-sheng jr*
没有香皂/卫生纸

The door does not close properly **Men guanbudao**
*men gwan-boo-dao*
门关不到

*Things to remember*

> In addition to the decimal metric system, the
> traditional units of measure are still used in China. You
> will need to get to grips with these if you intend to
> make your food purchases at the market.

## Weight

| | | |
|---|---|---|
| milligram | **haoke** (*hao-ke*) | 毫克 |
| gram | **ke** (*ke*) | 克 |
| 100 grams | **baike** (*bai-ke*) | 百克 |
| kilo | **gongjin** (*goong-jin*) | 公斤 |
| quintal | **bai gongjin** (*bai goong-jin*) | 百公斤 |
| ton | **dun** (*doon*) | 吨 |

## Chinese units of weight

| | | |
|---|---|---|
| **jin**<br>*jin* | 斤 | 500 g |
| **liang**<br>*liang* | 两 | 50 g |
| **qian**<br>*chien* | 钱 | 5 g |

## Length

| | | |
|---|---|---|
| millimeter | **haomi**<br>*hao-mee* | 毫米 |
| centimeter | **gongfen**<br>*goong-fen* | 公分 |
| meter | **mi**<br>*mee* | 米 |
| kilometer | **gongli**<br>*goong-lee* | 公里 |

## Chinese units of length

| | | |
|---|---|---|
| **cun**<br>*tsoon* | 寸 | 3,3 cm |
| **fen**<br>*fen* | 分 | 0,3 m |
| **chi**<br>*chr* | 尺 | 33,3 cm |
| **zhang**<br>*jang* | 丈 | 3,3 m |
| **li**<br>*lee* | 里 | 500 m |

# GASTRONOMIC
# DICTIONARY

*The long history of the Chinese language has given rise to a huge variety of expressions. Often there are numerous ways of saying the same thing, all of which are equally common; and so this Dictionary comprises the main synonyms of certain words.*

**above**上边 shangbian *shang-bien*

**additive** 添加剂 tianjiaji *tien-jia-jee*

**address** 地址 dizhi *dee-jr*

**adult** 大人 daren *da-ren*

**airplane** 飞机 feiji *fay-jee*

**airport** 飞机场 feijichang *fay-jee-chang*

**aftertaste** 余味 yuwei *yoo-way*

**again** 还 hai *hai*, 再 zai *dsai*

**air** 空气 kongqi *koong-chee*; **air conditioning** 空调 kongtiao *koong-tiao*

**alcoholic** 酒精 jiujing *jioh-jing*, 含酒精 hanjiujing *han-jioh-jing*

**all** 都 dou *doe*, suoyou 所有 *swo-yo*

**allergy** 过敏 guomin *gwo-min*

**almond** 杏仁 xingren *sing-ren*

**almost** 差不多 chabuduo *cha-boo-dwo*

**also** 也 ye *yeh*

**American** 美国人 meiguoren *may-gwo-ren* (native of the United States)

**anise** 茴 hui *hweh*; **aniseed** 八角 bajiao *ba-jiao*

**aperitif** 开胃酒 kaiweijiu *kai-way-jioh*

**appetite** 胃口 weikou *way-ko*

**appetizer** 酒菜 jiucai *jioh-tsai*, 拼盘 pinpan *pin-pan*

**apple** 苹果 pingguo *ping-gwo*

**appointment** 约会 yuehui *yweh-hwee*

**appreciate, to** 喜欢 xihuan *see-hwan*

**apricot** 杏 xing *sing*

**aroma** 口味 kouwei *ko-way*

**aromatic** 口味的 kouweide *ko-way-d*

**aromatic herbs** 芳草 fangcao *fang-tsao*

**arrive, to** 到达 daoda *dao-da*, 来到 laidao *lai-dao*

**artichoke** 洋蓟 yangji *yang-jee*

**ash tray** 烟灰缸 yanhuigang *yen-hweh-gang*

**asparagus** 芦笋 lusun *loo-soon*

**at least** 至少 zhishao *jr-shao*

**avocado** 油梨 youli *yo-lee*

**baby's feeding-bottle** 奶瓶 naiping *nai-ping*

**bacon** 咸肉 xianrou *sien-ro*

**bad** 坏 huai *hwai*, 不好 buhao *boo-hao*

**bag** 提包 tibao *tee-bao*

**baggage** 行李 xingli *sing-lee*, 箱子 xiangzi *siang-ds*

**baked** 烤的 kaode *kao-d*

**bamboo** 竹子 zhuzi *joo-ds*; **bamboo shoots** 笋 sun *soon*, 竹笋 zhusun *joo-soon*

**banana** 香蕉 xiangjiao *siang-jiao*

**bank** 银行 yinhang *yin-hang*

**banquet** 宴会 yanhui *yen-hweh*

**bar** 酒吧 jiuba *jioh-ba*, 咖啡馆 kafeiguan *ka-fay-gwan*

**barley** 大麦 damai *da-may*

**basil** 罗勒 luole *lwo-le*

**bass** 鲈鱼 luyu *loo-yoo*

**bean** 豆子 douzi *doe-ds*

**beansprouts** 豆芽 douya *doe-ya*

**beautiful** 美丽 meili *may-lee*, 漂亮 piaoliang *piao-liang*

**beef** 牛肉 niurou *niu-ro*

**beer** 啤酒 pijiu *pee-jioh*

**beet** 甜菜 tiancai *tien-tsai*

**Beijing** 北京 Beijing *bay-jing*

**berry** 聚合果 juheguo *joo-heh-gwo*

**beverage** 饮料 yinliao *yin-liao*; **nonalcoholic drink** 不含酒饮料 buhanjiu yinliao *boo-han-jioh yin-liao*; **fizzy drink** 呆气饮料 daiqi yinliao *dai-chee yin-liao*, 汽水 qishui *chee-shweh*

**big** 大da *da*

**bill** 帐单 zhangdan *jang-dan*

**biscuit** 饼干binggan *bing-gan*; **moon biscuits** 月饼 yuebing *yweh-bing*

**bitter** 味数 wei shu *way shoo*; 苦 ku *koo*; 酸suan *swan*

**bitter-sweet** 糖醋 tangcu *tang-tsoo*, 酸甜suantian *swan-tien*

**blueberry** 越橘 yueju *yweh-joo*

**boil, to** 煮 zhu *joo*; **boiled** 煮的 zhude *joo-d*

**boiling** 烫的 tangde *tang-d*

**bone** 骨 gu *goo*

**book, to** 顶 ding *ding*, yuding *yoo-ding*

**bottle** 瓶 ping *ping*; **bottled** 瓶装 pingzhuang *ping-jwang*; **bottle opener** 开瓶器 kaipingqi *kai-ping-chee*

**bowl** 碗wan *wan*

**brain** 脑子 naozi *nao-ds*

**braised** 红烧 hongshao *hong-shao*

**bread** 面包 mianbao *mien-bao*; **steamed bread** 馒头 mantou *man-toe*; **steamed filled bread** 包子 baozi *bao-ds*; **filled bread** 夹菜面包 jiacai mianbao *jia-tsai mien-bao*; **sesame bread** 烧饼 shaobing *shao-bing*; **leavened bread** 发面饼 famianbing *fa-mien-bing*; **sweet leavened bread** 小松饼 xiaosongbing *siao-soong-bing*

**breakfast** 早饭 zaofan *dsao-fan*; **Western-style breakfast** 西式早饭 xishi zaofan *see-shr dsao-fan*

**breed, to** 羊动物 yang dongwu *yang doong-woo*

**broad beans** 蚕豆 candou *tsan-doe*

**broccoli** 花椰采 huayecai *hwa-yeh-tsai*

**broken** 故障 guzhang *goo-jang*

**broth** 清汤 qingtang *ching-tang*, 原汤 yuantang *ywen-tang*; **meat broth**

肉汤 routang *ro-tang*

**brush** 刷子 shuazi *shwa-ds*

**buffet** 自主餐 zizhucan
*ds-joo-tsan*

**burned** 燃烧 ranshao
*ran-shao*, 烧伤
shaoshang *shao-shang*

**butcher** 肉商 roushang
*ro-shang*

**butter** 黄油 huangyou
*hwang-yo*; **yak's butter**
毛牛黄油 maoniu
huangyou *mao-niu
hwang-yo*

**bus** 公共汽车 gonggong
qiche *goong-goong
chee-che*

**buy, to** 买 mai *mai*

**cacao** 可可 keke *ke-ke*

**caffeine** 咖啡因 kafeiyin
*ka-fay-yin*

**cake** 蛋糕 dangao *dan-gao*,
糕饼 gaobing *gao-bing*

**call, to** 叫人 jiao ren
*jiao ren*

**calm** 按金 anjing
*an-jing*, 平金 pingjing
*ping-jing*

**calorie** 卡路里 kaluli
*ka-loo-lee*

**camomile** 春黄菊
chunhuangju
*choon-hwang-joo*

**can opener** 开罐器
kaiguanqi *kai-gwan-chee*

**cancel, to** 取消 quxiao
*choo-siao*

**candies** 蜜饯 mijian
*mee-jien*

**candy** 糖 tang *tang*

**canteen** 食堂 shitang *shr-tang*

**Canton** 广州 Guangzhou
*gwang-jo*

**capers** 续随子 xusuizi
*soo-sweh-ds*

**capo** 阉鸡 yanji *yen-jee*

**cappuccino** 卡普契诺咖啡
kapuqinuo kafei
*ka-poo-chee-nwo ka-fay*

**carafe** 水壶 shuihu
*shweh-hoo*

**caramel** 焦糖 jiaotang
*jiao-tang*; **caramelized**
拔丝 basi *ba-s*

**cardoon** 蓟 ji *jee*

**carrot** 红萝卜 hongluobo

*hong-lwo-boh*

**carp** 鲤鱼 liyu *lee-yoo*

**cash** 现钱 xianqian *sien-chien*

**cashew-nuts** 腰果 yaoguo *yao-gwo*

**cashier** 收款员 shoukuanyuan *sho-kwan-ywen*

**cauliflower** 采花 caihua *tsai-hwa*

**celery** 芹菜 qincai *chin-tsai*

**cereals** 粮食 liangshi *liang-shr*

**chair** 椅子 yizi *ee-ds*

**champagne** 香槟酒 xiangbingjiu *siang-bing-jioh*

**change** 找的钱 zhaodeqian *jao-d-chien*; **change, to** 改变 gaibian *gai-bien*, 变化 bianhua *bien-hwa*, 换 huan *hwan*

**chaperon** 领队 lingdui *ling-dweh*

**cheap** 便宜 bianyi *bien-ee*

**cheap, informal restaurant** 小吃店 xiaochidian *siao-chr-dien*

**check** 支票 zhipiao *jr-piao*; **check, to** 检查 jiancha *jien-cha*

**checkout** 收款处 shoukuanchu *sho-kwan-choo*

**cheers, your health** 干杯 ganbei *gan-bay*

**cheese** 奶酪 nailo *nai-loh*, 干酪 ganlao *gan-lao*

**cherry** 樱桃 yingtao *ying-tao*

**chew, to** 嚼 jiao *jiao*

**chewing gum** 口香糖 kouxiangtang *ko-siang-tang*

**chicken** 鸡 ji *jee*; **chicken with almonds** gongbao jiding *goong-bao jee-ding* 宫保鸡丁; **chicken with lemon** 西拧蒴片 xining jipian *see-ning jee-pien*

**chick-peas** 鹰嘴豆 yingzuidou *ying-dsweh-doe*

**chicory** 菊苣 juju *joo-joo*

**child** 孩子 haizi *hai-ds*

**chili pepper** 辣椒 lajiao *la-jiao*

**China** 中国 Zhongguo
*joong-gwo*
**Chinese** (language) 汉语
hanyu *han-yoo*; (native of
China) 中国人
zhongguoren
*joong-gwo-ren*; **Mandarin
Chinese** 普通话
putonghua *poo-dong-hwa*
**Chinese cabbage** 白菜
baicai *bai-tsai*
**Chinese characters** 汉子
hanzi *han-ds*
**chocolate** 巧克力 qiaokeli
*chiao-ke-lee*
**chop** 排骨 paigu *pai-goo*;
**porkchop** 猪肉排骨
zhurou paigu *joo-ro
pai-goo*
**chopsticks** 筷子 kuaizi
*kwai-ds*
**cigar** 雪茄 xueqie
*sweh-chie*
**cigarette** 香烟 xiangyan
*siang-yen*
**cinnamon** 桂皮 guipi
*gweh-pee*
**citrus fruit** 杆橘水果
ganju shuiguo *gan-joo*

*shweh-gwo*
**citrus tree** 拘橼 juyuan
*joo-ywen*
**city** 城市 chengshi
*cheng-shr*
**clean** 干净 ganjing
*gan-jing*
**cloakroom** 衣帽间
yimaojian *ee-mao-jien*
**close, to** 关门 guangmen
*gwang-men*; **closed** 关
guang *gwang*
**cloves** 丁香 dingxiang
*ding-siang*
**Coca-Cola** 可口可乐
kekou kele *ke-ko ke-le*
**cockerel** 鸡 ji *jee*
**coconut** 椰子 yezi *yeh-ds*
**cod** 鳕鱼 xueyu
*sweh-yoo*
**coffee** 咖啡 kafei *ka-fay*;
**black coffee** 黑咖啡
heikafei *hay-ka-fay*;
**decaffeinated
coffee** 除去咖啡因的
chuqu kafeiyinde *choo-
choo kafay-yin-d*
**coffee cup** 杯 bei *bay*
**cognac** 法国白兰地

faguo bailandi *fa-gwo bai-lan-dee*

**cold** 冷 leng *leng*

**cold sliced meat** 拼盘 pinpan *pin-pan*

**color** 颜色 yanse *yen-s*

**comfortable** 舒服 shufu *shoo-foo*

**complaint** 投诉 tousu *toe-soo*

**compulsory** 必须作的 bixuzuode *bee-soo-dswo-d*

**condiment** 调味料 tiaoweiliao *tiao-way-liao*, 作料 zuoliao *dswo-liao*

**confectionery** 唐代店 tiandian *tien-dien*

**confirm, to** 确认 queren *chweh-ren*

**Confucius** 孔子 Kongzi *koong-ds*

**cook** 厨师 chushi *choo-shr*

**cook, to** 作饭 zuofan *dswo-fan*; 煮 zhu *joo*; **cooked** 煮的 zhude *joo-d*

**cooking** 烹调 pengtiao *peng-tiao*

**coquille St. Jacques** 扇贝 shanbei *shan-bay*

**coriander** 芫荽 yansui *yen-sweh*, 香菜 xiangcai *siang-tsai*

**cork** 瓶塞 pingsai *ping-sai*

**corkscrew** 开瓶器 kaipingqi *kai-ping-chee*

**corn** 玉米 yumi *yoo-mee*

**cornflakes** 玉米片 yumipian *yoo-mee-pien*

**cornstarch** 玉米粉 yumifen *yoo-mee-fen*

**courgette** 菜瓜 caigua *tsai-gwa*

**course** 采 cai *tsai*

**crab** 螃蟹 pangxie *pang-sie*

**cream** 奶油 naiyou *nai-yo*

**credit card** 信用卡 xinyongka *sin-yong-ka*

**crisp** 脆 cui *tsweh*, 酥 su *soo*

**croissant** 新月形 面包 xinyuexing mianbao *sin-yweh-sing mien-bao*

**crowded** 挤 ji *jee*

**crustaceans** 水蛇 有壳动物 shuisheng youqiao dongwu *shweh-sheng yo-chiao*

*dong-woo*
**cucumber** 黄瓜 huanggua
*hwang-gwa*
**cuisine** 烹调 pengtiao
*peng-tiao;* **Chinese cuisine**
中餐 zhongcan *joong-tsan;*
**Western cuisine** 西餐
xican *see-tsan*
**cumin** 欧式采 oushicai
*oe-shr-tsai*
**cup** 碗 wan *wan*
**currant** 黑醋栗 heicuili
*hay-tsoo-lee*
**currency** 硬币 yingbi
*ying-bee;* 货币 houbi
*ho-bee,* waihui 外汇
*wai-hweh;* **currency**
**exchange** 对换 duihuan
*dweh-hwan*
**curry** 咖哩 gali *ga-lee*
**custard** 奶油 naiyou
*nai-yo*
**custodian** 看门人
kanmenren *kan-men-ren*
**customer** 顾客 guke *goo-ke*
**cut, to** 切 qie *cie*
**cutlery** 餐具 canju *tsan-joo,*
刀叉 daocha *dao-cha*
**cutlet** 排骨 paigu *pai-goo*

**cuttlefish** 墨斗鱼
modouyu *moh-doe-yoo*

**dairy products** 乳制品
ruzhipin *roo-jr-pin*
**dark** 深 shen *shen*
**date** 枣子 zaozi *dsao-ds*
**debit, to** 要钱 yaoqian
*yao-chien*
**delay** 晚 wan *wan*
**delicious** 非常好吃
feichang haochi *fay-chang*
*hao-chr*
**deer** 鹿 lu *loo*
**deposit** 定金 dingjin
*ding-jin*
**depot** 预付 yufu *yoo-foo*
**diabetes** 糖尿病
tangniaobing
*tang-niao-bing;* **diabetic**
糖尿病患者 tangniaobing
huanzhe *tang-niao-bing*
*hwan-j*
**diet** 食物 shiwu
*shr-woo;* 介质饮食 jiezhi
yinshi *jie-jr yin-shr;* 节食
jieshi *jie-shr*
**different** 不一样的
bu yiyangde *boo ee-yang-d*

**digestible** 好消化
haoxiaohua *hao-siao-hwa*
**digestion** 消化 xiaohua
*siao-hwa*
**digestive** 助消化
zhuxiaohua *joo-siao-hwa*
**dining room** 饭厅 fanting
*fan-ting*
**dinner** 晚饭 wanfan
*wan-fan*
**direction** 方向 fangxian
*fang-sian*
**director** 经理 jingli
*jing-lee*
**dirty** 脏 zang *dsang*
**dish** 盘子 panzi *pan-ds*
**document** 文件 wenjian
*wen-jien*,证明
zhengming *jeng-ming*
**donut** 炸圆饼 zhayuanbing
*ja-ywen-bing*
**door** 门 men *men*
**drink, to** 喝 he *heh*
**dry** 干燥 ganzao *gantsao*;
干 gan *gan*
**duck** 鸭 ya *ya*; **Peking
crispy duck** 北京烤鸭
Beijing kaoya *bay-jing
kao-ya*

**ear** (cereal) 玉米梆子 yumi
bangzi *yoo-mee bang-ds*
**eat, to** 吃饭 chifan
*chr-fan*
**eel** 鳗鲡 manli
*man-lee*
**egg** 鸡蛋 jidan *jee-dan*;
**boiled eggs** 半熟鸡蛋
banshudan *ban-shoo-dan*;
**eggs of the 100 years**
百年鸡蛋 bainian jidan
*bai-nien jee-dan*; **fried
eggs** 荷包蛋 hebaodan
*heh-bao-dan*; **hard-boiled
eggs** 煮鸡蛋 zhu jidan
*joo jee-dan*; **scrambled
egg** 吵蛋 chaodan
*chao-dan*; **egg white**蛋清
danqing *dan-ching*; **egg
yolk** 蛋黄 danhuang *dan-
hwang*
**eggplant** 茄子qiezi *chie-ds*
**elevator** 电梯 dianti
*dien-tee*
**embassy** 大使馆
dashiguan *da-shr-gwan*
**emperor** 皇帝 huangdi
*hwang-dee*
**empty** 空 kong *koong*

**endive** 苣荬菜 jumaicai
*joo-mai-tsai*

**engaged** (with reference to a person) 忙 mang *mang*;
**the toilet is engaged** 厕所正用得 cesuo zhengyongzhi *tse-swo jan-yong-jr*

**English** (language) 英语 yingyu *ying-yoo*; (native of Great Britain) 英国人 yingguoren *ying-gwo-ren*

**enjoy your meal!** 胃口好 weikouhao *way-ko-hao*

**enough** 足够 zugou *dsoo-go*

**entrails** 内脏 neizang *nay-dsang*; 脏器 zangqi *dsang-chee*

**entrance** 入口 rukou *roo-ko*

**envelope** 信奉 xinfeng *sin-feng*

**equal** 一样的 yiyangde *ee-yang-de*

**evening** 晚上 wanshang *wan-shang*

**excursion** 游览 youlan *yo-lan*, 郊游 jiaoyou *jiao-yo*

**exit** 出口 chukou *choo-ko*

**expensive** 贵 gui *gweh*

**family** 家 jia *jia*

**fast** 快 kuai *kwai*

**fast-food** 快餐店 kuaicandian *kwai-tsan-dien*

**fat** 肥 fei *fay*

**fennel** 茴香 huixiang *hweh-siang*

**ferment, to** 酿造 niangzao *niang-dsao*; **fermented** 酿造的 niangzaode *niang-dsao-d*

**fig** 无花果 wuhuaguo *woo-hwa-gwo*

**filled** 夹馅 jiaxian *jia-sien*; **filled parcel** 卷儿 juar *jwar*

**fillet** 里脊 liji *lee-jee*

**filling** 陷 xian *sien*

**fire** 火 huo *hwo*

**fish** 鱼 yu *yoo*,鱼肉 yurou *yooro*

**fishing** 钓鱼 diaoyu *diao-yoo*

**five-spice powder** 五香粉 wuxiangfen *woo-siang-fen*

**fizzy** 呆气 daiqi
*dai-chee*

**flame** 火焰 huoyan
*hwo-yen*

**flavor, to** 加调味 jia
tiaowei *jia tiao-way*

**floor** 楼 lou *lo*

**flour** 面粉 mianfen
*mien-fen*; **rice flour** 米粉
mifen *mee-fen*

**"focaccia bread"** 烤饼
kaobing *kao-bing*, 烤面饼
kaomianbing
*kao-mien-bing*

**food** 食品 shipin *shr-pin*;
**Chinese food** 中彩
zhongcai *joong-tsai*;
**Western food** 西餐
xicai *see-tsai*

**food poisoning** 食物中毒
shiwu zhongdu *shr-woo
joong-doo*

**foot** 脚 jiao *jiao*; **on foot**
走路 zoulu *dso-loo*

**foreigner** 外国人
waiguoren *wai-gwo-ren*

**fork** 叉子 chazi *cha-ds*

**France** 法国 Faguo *fa-gwo*

**free** 免费 mianfei *mien-fay*

**French** (language) 法语
fayu *fa-yoo*; (native of
France) 法国人 faguoren
*fa-gwo-ren*

**fresh** 新鲜 xinxian
*sin-sien*

**fried** 炸 zha *ja*, 煎
jian *jien*

**fried potato balls** 炸丸子
zhawanzi *ja-wan-ds*

**fried wonton** 吵馄钝 chao
hundun *chao hoon-doon*

**friend** 朋友 pengyou
*peng-yo*

**fritter** 饺子 jiaozi *jiao-ds*

**frog** 青蛙 qingwa *ching-wa*

**fruit** 水果 shuiguo *shweh-
gwo*; **fresh fruit**
鲜水果 xian shuiguo *sien
shweh-gwo*; **dried fruit**
干水果 gan shuiguo *gan
shweh-gwo*; **fruit that is
fried and caramelized**
拔丝水果 basi shuiguo
*ba-s shweh-gwo*; **fruit
salad** 水果沙粒 shuiguo
shala *shweh-gwo sha-la*

**frying pan** 煎锅 jianguo
*jien-gwo*

**game** (poultry) 野味 yewei
*yeh-way*

**garlic** 大蒜 dasuan
*da-swan*

**gas station** 加油站
jiayouzhan *jia-yo-jan*

**gastronomy** 烹任 pengren
*peng-ren*

**gentleman** 先生 xiansheng
*sien-sheng*

**gherkin** 小黄瓜
xiaohuanggua
*siao-hwang-gwa*

**gin** 杜松酒 dusongzijiu
*doo-soong-ds-jioh*

**ginger** 生姜 shengjiang
*sheng-jiang*

**ginseng** 人参 renshen
*ren-shen*

**glass** 杯子 beizi
*bay-ds*

**go out, to** 出去 chuqu
*choo-choo*, 出来 chulai
*choo-lai*

**go up, to** 上 shang *shang*,
登 deng *deng*

**good** 好 hao *hao*

**goose** 鹅 e *e*

**grapefruit** 柚子 youzi
*yo-ds*

**grapes** 葡萄 putao *poo-tao*

**grappa** 白兰地 bailandi
*bai-lan-dee*

**greasy** 油泥 youni *yo-nee*

**Great Britain** 英国
Yingguo *ying-gwo*

**green** 绿 lu *loo*

**grill** 考绩 kaojia *kao-jia*;
**grilled** 烤 kao *kao*; 考绩的
kaojiade *kao-jia-d*

**grocery store** 食品商店
shipin shangdian
*shr-pin shang-dien*

**group** 团 tuan *twan*,
组 zu *dsoo*

**group leader** 领队
lingdui *ling-dweh*

**grow, to** 羊动物 yang
dongwu *yang doong-woo*

**guide** (person) 向导
xiangdao *siang-dao*; (book)
指南 zhinan *jr-nan*

**hake** 黑线鳕 heixianxue
*hay-sien-sweh*

**ham** 火腿 huotui *hwo-tweh*

**handbag** 手提包 shoutibao
*sho-tee-bao*

**hare** 兔子 tuzi *too-ds*

**have, to** 有 you *yo*

**hazelnut** 榛子 zhenzi *jen-ds*

**heat, to** 加热 jiare *jia-r*

**heating** 暖气 nuanqi *nwan-chee*

**heavy** 重 zhong *joong*

**help, to** 帮助 bangzhu *bang-joo*

**hen** 母鸡 muji *moo-jee*

**here** 在这儿 zai zher *dsai jer*

**herring** 鲱鱼 feiyu *fay-yoo*

**highchair** 糕脚椅 gaojiaoyi *gao-jiao-ee*

**holiday** 假日 jiari *jia-r*

**honey** 蜂蜜 fengmi *feng-mee*

**Hong Kong** 香港 Xianggang *siang-gang*

**horseradish** 萝卜 luobo *lwo-boh*

**hot** 热 re *re*

**hotel** 饭店 fandian *fan-dien*

**hour** 小时 xiaoshi *siao-shr*

**how much** (large quantities) 多少 duoshao *dwo-shao*; (small quantities) 几个 jige *jee-g*

**hunger** 饥饿 jie *jie*, 饿 e *e*

**ice** 冰 bing *bing*; **ice cube** 冰块 bingkuair *bing-kwair*

**ice-cream** 冰淇淋 bingqiling *bing-chee-ling*

**ice-cream parlor** 冰淇淋店 bingqilingdian *bing-chee-ling-dien*

**ice-lolly** 冰棍 binggunr *bing-goor*

**icing** 糖衣 tangyi *tang-ee*

**ideogram** 汉字 hanzi *han-ds*

**included** 包括 baokuo *bao-kwo*

**indigestion** 消化不食 xiaohua bushi *siao-hwa boo-shr*

**infusion** 茶 cha *cha*

**ingredient** 原料 yuanliao *ywen-liao*, 作料 zuoliao *dswo-liao*

**invite, to** 请 qing *ching*

**Italian** (language of Italy)

意大利语 yidaliyu *ee-da-lee-yoo*; (native of Italy) 意大利人 yidaliren *ee-da-lee-ren*

**Italy** 意大利 Yidali *ee-da-lee*

**jackdaw** 豆角 doujiao *doe-jiao*

**jam** 果酱 guojiang *gwo-jiang*

**jasmine** 茉莉花 molihua *moh-lee-hwa*

**jelly** 果冻 guodong *gwo-doong*

**juice** 汁 zhi *jr*; **orange juice** 桔汁 juzhi *joo-jr*; **fruit juice** 果汁 guozhi *gwo-jr*

**kid** (baby goat) 小山羊 xiaoshanyang *siao-shan-yang*

**kidney** 肾 shen *shen*, 肾脏 shenzang *shen-dsang*

**kitchen** 厨房 chufan *choo-fan*

**kiwi** 猕猴桃 mihoutao *mee-ho-tao*

**knife** 刀子 daozi *dao-ds*

**ladle** 长勺 changshao *chang-shao*

**lady** 太太 taitai *tai-tai*, 女士 nushi *noo-shr*

**lamb** 羊 yang *yang*

**lamp** 灯 deng *deng*

**lard** 荤油 hunyou *hoon-yo*

**large** 大 da *da*

**laurel** 肉桂 rougui *ro-gweh*, 月桂 yuegui *yweh-gweh*

**lay the table, to** 摆桌子 bai zhuozi *bai jwo-ds*

**lean** 瘦 shou *sho*

**leg** 退 tui *tweh*, 爪子 zhuazi *jwa-ds*

**leek** 大葱 dacong *da-tsong*

**lemon** 柠檬 ningmeng *ning-meng*

**lemonade** 柠檬汽水 ningmeng qishui *ning-meng chee-shweh*

**lentils** 小扁豆 xiaobiandou *siao-bien-doe*

**lettuce** 沙粒 shala *sha-la*, 莴苣 woju *woh-joo*

**light** 轻 qing *ching*

**lily** 百合 baihe *bai-heh*

**liquid** 液体 yeti *yeh-tee*

**liqueur** 白酒 baijiu *bai-jioh*

**liquorice** 甘草 gancao *gan-tsao*

**liter** 升sheng *sheng;* **one liter** 一升 yisheng *ee-sheng*

**little** 少 shao *shao*,不多 buduo *boo-dwo*

**liver** 肝 gan *gan*

**lobster** 龙虾 longxia *long-sia*

**local** 本份的 benfangde *ben-fang-d*

**loin** 腰肉 yaorou *yao-ro*

**London** 伦敦 Lundun *loon-doon*

**long (thin) strips of pasta** 切面 qiemian *chie-mien*

**lotus** 莲花 lianhua *lien-hwa;* **lotus leaves** 荷叶 heye *heh-yeh;* **lotus root** 莲蓬 lianpeng *lien-peng;* **lotus seeds** 莲子 lianzi *lien-ds*

**lunch** 午饭 wufan *woo-fan*

**lychee** 荔枝 lizhi *lee-jr*

**lychum** 构杞子 gouqizi *go-chee-ds*

**mahjong** 麻将 majiang *ma-jiang*

**management** 管理处 guanlichu *gwan-lee-choo*

**mandarin** (fruit) 桔子 juzi *joo-ds;* (official) 管理 guanli *gwan-lee;* (language) 普通话 putonghua *poo-tong-hwa*

**mango** 茫果 mangguo *mang-gwo*

**marinated** 腌泡 yanpao *yen-pao*

**market** 自由市场 ziyou shichang *ds-yo shr-chang*

**meal** 饭食 fanshi *fan-shr*

**meat** 肉 rou *ro;* **canned meat** 罐头肉 guantourou *gwan-toe-ro;* **minced meat** 肉松 rousong *ro-soong*

**meatball** 丸子 wanzi *wan-ds*

**medlar** 批杷 pipa *pee-pa*

**melon** 西瓜 xigua *see-gwa*

**menu** 菜单 caidan *tsai-dan;* **fixed-price menu** 套餐 taocan *tao-tsan*

**milk** 牛奶 niunai *niu-nai;* **powdered milk**

奶粉 naifen *nai-fen*

**millet** 小米 xiaomi *siao-mee*

**mince, to** 切 qie *chie*

**mint** 薄荷 bohe *boh-heh*

**minute** 分钟 fenzhong
*fen-joong*

**mixed** 什锦 shijin *shr-jin*

**mixture** 混合 hunhe
*hoon-heh*

**mollusk** 软体动物 ruanti
dongwu *rwan-tee
dong-woo*

**Mongolian fondu** 火锅
huoguo *hwo-gwo,* 刷羊肉
shuanyangrou *shwan-
yang-ro*

**monosodium glutamate**
味精 weijing *way-jing*

**monument** 纪年碑
jinianbei *jee-nien-bay*

**morsel** 小块 xiaokuai
*siao-kwai,* 少量
shaoliang *shao-liang*

**mosquito** 蚊子 wenzi
*wen-ds*

**mouth** 口 kou *ko*

**mullet** 鲻鱼 ziyu *ds-yoo*

**museum** 博物馆 bowuguan
*boh-woo-gwan*

**mushroom** 蘑菇 mogu
*moh-goo;* **fresh**
**mushrooms** 鲜蘑菇 xian
mogu *sien moh-goo;* **dried**
**mushrooms** 干蘑菇 gan
mogu *gan moh-goo*

**mussels** 淡菜 dancai
*dan-tsai*

**mustard** 芥菜 jiecai
*jie-tsai,* 芥末 jiemo
*jie-moh*

**mutton** 山羊 shanyang
*shan-yang*

**Nanking** 南京 Nanjing
*nan-jing*

**name** 名字 mingzi *ming-ds*

**napkin** 餐巾 canjin *tsan-jin,*
面纸 mianzhi *mien-jr*

**nation** 国家 guojia
*gwo-jia*

**need, to** 需要 xuyao
*soo-yao*

**New York** 纽约 Niuyue
*niu-yweh*

**nibble** 点心 dianxin *dien-
sin*

**noise** 吵 chao *chao*

**noisy** 吵的 chaode *chao-d*

**nonalcoholic** 不含酒精的
buhan jiujingde *boo-han
jioh-jing-d*, 软饮料
ruanyinliao *rwan-yin-liao*

**noodles** 面条 miantiao
*mien-tiao*; **rice noodles**
米粉 mifen *mee-fen*; **fried
noodles** 炒面 chaomian
*chao-mien*

**not** 不 bu *boo*

**now** 现在 xianzai *sien-dsai*

**number** 号 hao *hao*, 号码
haoma *hao-ma*

**nut** 核桃 hetao *heh-tao*

**nutcracker** 核桃夹
hetaojia *heh-tao-jia*

**nutmeg** 豆蔻 doukou *doe-ko*

**nutritious** 有营养
youyingyang *yo-ying-yang*

**oats** 燕麦 yanmai
*yen-mai*

**oil** 油 you *yo*; **chili oil**
辣椒油 lajiaoyou
*la-jiao-yo*; **peanut oil**
花生油 huashengyou
*hwa-sheng-yo*; **sesame oil**
脂麻油 zhimayou *jr-ma-yo*

**old** 老 lao *lao*

**olive** 甘蓝 ganlan *gan-lan*

**omelet** 煎蛋卷 jian
danjuanr *jien dan-jwar*

**onion** 葱 cong *tsong*

**open** 开着的 kaizhede
*kai-j-de*; **open, to** 打开
dakai *da-kai*

**orange** 橙子 chenzi
*chen-ds*; **orange juice**
桔子水 juzishui
*joo-ds-shweh*

**order** 定做 dingzuo
*ding-dswo*; **order, to** 定
ding *ding*, 要 yao *yao*

**other** 其他 qita *chee-ta*

**out of order** 不行 buxing
*boo-sing*

**outside, in the open air**
户外 huwai *hoo-wai*

**oven** 沪 hu *hoo*

**ox** 牛 niu *niu*

**oyster** 蚝 hao *hao*

**pan** 锅 guo *gwo*, 煎锅
jianguo *jien-gwo*; **roasting
pan** 烤盘 kaopan *kao-pan*

**pancakes** 油煎饼
youjianbing *yo-jien-bing*;
煎饼 jianbing *jien-bing*

**papaya** 木瓜 mugua
*moo-gwa*

**paper** 纸 zhi *jr*; **toilet paper**
卫生纸 weishengzhi
*way-sheng-jr*; **paper**
**handkerchief** 面纸
mianzhi *mien-jr*

**Paris** 巴黎 Bali *ba-lee*

**parking** 停车站
tingchezhang *ting-che-jang*

**parsley** 欧芹采 ouqincai
*oe-chin-tsai*, 香菜
xiangcai *siang-tsai*

**passport** 护照 huzhao *hu-jao*

**pasta** 面食 mianshi
*mien-shr*, 面条 miantiao
*mien-tiao*; **sweet soya**
**paste** 甜面酱 tianmian
jiang *tien-mien jiang*

**patisserie** 糕点店
gaodiandian *gao-dien-dien*

**pay, to** 付款 fukuan
*foo-kwan* 支 zhi *jr*

**payment** 支付 zhifu
*jr-foo*, 付款 fukuan *foo-kwan*

**pea** 豌豆 wandou
*wan-doe*

**peach** 桃 tao *tao*

**peanuts** 花生 huasheng
*hwa-sheng*

**pear** 利li *lee*

**peel** 皮pi *pee*; **peel, to** 剥皮
bopi *boh-pee*, 削皮 xuepi
*sweh-pee*

**pepper** 胡椒粉 hujiaofen
*hoo-jiao-fen*, 大椒 dajiao
*da-jiao*; **Sichuan pepper**
(or **Chinese red pepper**)
花椒 huajiao *hwa-jiao*

**pepper grinder** 胡椒磨
hujiaomo *hoo-jiao-moh*

**People's Republic of China**
中国人民共和国
Zhongguo renmin
gongheguo *joong-gwo*
*ren-min goong-heh-gwo*

**Pepsi-Cola** 白事可乐
baishi kele *bai-shr ke-le*

**perch** 鲈 lu *loo*

**performance** 节目 jiemu
*jie-moo*

**persimmon** 柿子 shizi
*shr-ds*

**pharmacy** 药店 yaodian
*yao-dien*

**pheasant** 贝母鸡 beimuji

*bay-moo-jee*

**pickles** 泡菜 paocai
*pao-tsai*

**pie** 果酱蛋糕 guojiang
dangao *gwo-jiang dan-gao*

**pie-dish** 烤盘 kaopan
*kao-pan*

**piece** 块 kuair *kwair;* **a piece**
一块 yi kuair *ee kwair*

**piece of toasted bread**
烤面包丁 kaomianbao
ding *kao-mien-bao ding*

**pigeon** 鸽子 gezi *ge-ds*

**pike** 狗鱼 gouyu *go-yoo*

**pillow** 枕头 zhentou *jen-toe*

**pineapple** 菠萝 boluo
*boh-lwo*

**pistachio** 开心果 kaixinguo
*kai-sin-gwo*

**place** 地方 difang *dee-fang*

**plum** 李子 lizi *lee-ds*

**pod** 豆皮 doupi *doe-pee*

**pomegranate** 石榴 shiliu
*shr-liu*

**porridge** 粥 zhou *jo*

**pork** 猪肉 zhurou *joo-ro;*
**sweet and sour pork**
古老肉 gulaorou
*goo-lao-ro;* **golden piglet**

金猪 jinzhu *jin-joo*

**portion** 份 fen *fen*

**postage stamp** 邮票
youpiao *ioou-piao*

**postcard** 明信片
mingxinpian *ming-sin-pien*

**potato** 土豆 tudou *too-doe;*
马铃薯 malingshu
*ma-ling-shoo;* **sweet
potatoes** 白薯 baishu
*bai-shoo;* **fried potatoes**
炸土豆 zha tudou *ja
too-doe*

**prawn** 打虾 daxia *da-sia*

**prefer, to** 更喜欢 geng
xihuan *geng see-hwan*

**premises** 店 dian *dien*

**prescription** 药方
yaofangi *yahoo-fan*

**preservative** 保护剂
baohuji *bao-hoo-jee*

**price** 价钱 jiaqian
*jia-chien*

**pudding** 布丁 buding
*boo-ding*

**pulp** 肉 rou *ro*

**pumpkin** 南瓜 nangua
*nan-gwa*

**Pinyin** 拼音 pin-yin *pin-yin*

**quail** 鹌鹑 anchun
*an-choon*

**queue** 尾巴 weiba *way-ba*

**rabbit** 兔子 tuzi *too-ds*

**radio** 收音机 shouyinji
*sho-yin-jee*

**radish** 萝卜 luobo
*lwo-boh*

**raisins** 葡萄干 putaogan
*poo-tao-gan*

**raspberry** 山莓 shanmei
*shan-may*

**ravioli** 饺子 jiaozi *jiao-ds*;
**boiled ravioli** 水饺
shuijiao *shweh-jiao*;
**stir-fried ravioli** 锅贴饺
guotie jiao *gwo-tieh jiao*

**raw** 生的 shengde *sheng-d*,
没熟的 meishude *may-shoo-d*

**ready** 准备好 zhunbeihao
*joon-bay-hao*

**receipt** 发票 fapiao
*fa-piao*

**recipe** 烹调法 pengtiaofa
*peng-tiao-fa*

**red** 红 hong *hong*

**red mullet** 绯鲤 feili *fay-lee*

**refrigerator** 冰箱
bingxiang *bing-siang*

**reimbursement** 退回
tuihui *tweh-hweh*

**rental** 出租 chuzu
*choo-dsoo*

**reservation** 顶 ding *ding*,
预定 yuding *yoo-ding*

**reserved** 预定的
yudingde *yoo-ding-d*

**restaurant** 饭馆 fanguan
*fan-gwan*, 餐厅 canting
*tsan-ting*, 酒店 jiudian
*jioh-dien*; **restaurant that
serves crispy duck** 烤鸭店
kaoyadian *kao-ya-dien*;
**vegetarian restaurant**
蔬菜馆 shucaiguan *shoo-tsai-gwan*

**rice** 大米 dami *da-mee*;
**boiled rice** 米饭 mifan
*mee-fan*; **fried rice**
锅巴 guoba *gwo-ba*;
**glutinous rice** 粘米
nianmi *nien-mee*;
**Cantonese stir-fried rice**
广东炒饭 Guangdong
chaofan *gwang-doong
chao-fan*; **rice noodles**

米粉 mifen *mee-fen*

**ripe** 熟 shu *shoo*

**roast** 烤 kao *kao*; **roasted** 烤的 kaode *kao-d*

**Rome** 罗马 Luoma *lwo-ma*

**room** 房间 fangjian *fang-jien*

**rose** 玫瑰 meigui *may-gweh*

**rosemary** 迷迭香 midiexiang *mee-die-siang*

**rotating serving platform** 转盘 zhuanpan *jwan-pan*

**rum** 甜酒 tianjiu *tien-jioh*

**saffron** 番红花 fanhonghua *fan-hong-hwa*

**sage** 鼠尾草 shuweicao *shoo-way-tsao*

**salmon** 鲑鱼 guiyu *gweh-yoo*; **smoked salmon** 熏鲑鱼 xun guiyu *soon gweh-yoo*

**salt** 盐巴 yanba *yen-ba*

**salt cellar** 盐缸 yangang *yen-gang*

**salty** 咸 xian *sien*

**same** 一样的 yiyangde *ee-yang-de*, 同一的 tongyide *tong-ee-d*

**sardine** 沙丁鱼 shadingyu *sha-ding-yoo*

**sauce** 酱 jiang *jiang*; **sweet and sour sauce** 甜酸酱 tiansuan jiang *tien-swan jiang*; **fish-flavored sauce** 鱼香油 yuxiangyou *yoo-siang yo*; **sweet bean sauce** 红豆沙 hongdou sha *hong-doe sha*; **spicy bean sauce** 辣豆瓣酱 ladouban jiang *la-doe-ban jiang*; **oyster sauce** 蚝油 haoyou *hao-yo*; **sesame sauce** 麻酱 majiang *ma-jiang*; **Hoisin sauce** 海鲜酱 haixianjiang *hai-sien-jiang*

**saucepan** 烧锅 shaoguo *shao-gwo*

**sausage** 香肠 xiangchang *siang-chang*; 肉食 roushi *ro-shr*

**sea** 海 hai *hai*, 海边 haibian *hai-bien*

**sea bream** 鲷鱼 diaoyu *diao-yoo*

**seafood** 海鲜 haixian *hai-sien*

**self-service** 自主式

zizhushi *ds-joo-shr*

**service** 服务 fuwu *foo-woo*

**sesame** 芝麻 zhima *jr-ma*

**shake** 果枝 guozhi *gwo-jr*

**sheet** 卷儿 juanr *jwar*

**shell, to** 除壳 chuke *choo-ke*

**shopping** 开销 kaixiao *kai-siao*; **to do the shopping** 买东西 mai dongxi *mai doong-see*

**show, to** 肩 biaoshi *biao-shr*, 表示 zhishi *jr-shr*

**shrimp** 指示 xia *sia*

**shoulder** 虾 jian *jien*

**signature** 签名 qianming *chien-ming*

**simple** 简单 jiandan *jien-dan*

**sirloin** 牛肉排骨 niurou paigu *niu-ro pai-goo*

**skewer** 串 chuan *chwan*

**slice** 块 kuai *kwai*

**slow, slowly** 慢慢地 manmandi *man-man-dee*

**small** 小 xiao *siao*

**smell** 味 wei *way*

**smoke, to** 吸烟 xiyan *see-yen*; **smoked** 熏 xun

soon

**snack** 点心 dianxin *dien-sin*

**snail** 蜗牛 woniu *woh-niu*

**snake** 蛇 she *shr*

**soap** 肥皂 feizao *fay-dsao*

**soft** 松软 songruan *soong-rwan*

**sole** 平鱼 pingyu *ping-yoo*

**some** 有的 youde *yo-d*

**sorghum** 高粱 gaoliang *gao-liang*

**soup** 汤 tang *tang*, 羹 geng *geng*, 农菜汤 nongcaitang *nong- tsai-tang*

**soup tureen** 汤碗 tangwan *tang-wan*

**soy sauce** 酱油 jiangyou *jiang-yo*; **soy sauce with mushrooms** 草菇老抽 caogu laochou *tsao-goo lao-cho*; **light soy sauce** 生抽王 shengchou wang *sheng-cho wang*; **spicy soy sauce** 辣酱 lajiang *la-jiang*; **dark soy sauce** 老抽王 laochou wang *lao-cho wang*

**soya** 大豆 dadou *da-doe*

**soya cheese** 豆腐 doufu
*toe-foo*

**sparkling** 呆气 daiqi
*dai-chee*; **sparkling wine**
汽酒 qijiu *chee-jioh*

**specialty** 特产 techan
*te-chan*

**spice** 作料 zuoliao
*dswo-liao*

**spicy** 辣 la *la*; **spicy and
sour** 酸辣 suanla *swan-la*

**spinach** 菠菜 bocai
*boh-tsai*

**spirit** 烈酒 liejiu *lie-jioh*,
烧酒 shaojiu *shao-jioh*

**spit** 烤钎 kaoqian
*kao-chien*

**spit-roasted** 串 chuan
*chwan*

**spring onion** 春葱
chuncong *choon-tsong*

**spring roll** 春卷儿
chunjuar *choon-jwar*

**squid** 鱿鱼 youyu
*yo-yoo*

**stairs** 梯 ti *tee*

**station** 车站 chezhan
*che-jan*; **railroad station**

火车站 huo chezhan
*hwo-che-jan*

**steak** 牛排 niupai
*niu-pai*

**steam** 蒸汽 zhengqi
*jeng-chee*; **steaming** 蒸
zheng *jeng*

**stew** 炖 dun *doon*

**stir-fry, to** 钞 chao *chao*

**stock cube** 味精 weijing
*way-jing*

**stop** 站 zhan *jan*

**strawberry** 草煤 caomei
*tsao-may*

**street** 路 lu *loo*

**string bean** 扁豆 biandou
*bien-doe*

**strong** (flavor) 味重
weizhong *way-joong*

**suitcase** 箱子 xiangzi
*siang-ds*

**sugar** 糖 tang *tang*

**sugar basin** 糖罐
tangguang *tang-gwang*

**supermarket** 超级市场
chaoji shichang *chao-jee
shr-chang*

**surname** 性 xing *sing*

**sweet** (adj.) 甜 tian *tien*;

(noun)甜点 tiandian
*tien-dien*; 糕点 gaodian
*gao-dien*

**sweetner** 唐代 tangdai
*tang-dai*

**swimming pool** 游泳池
youyongchi *yo-yong-chr*

**swordfish** 箭鱼 jianyu
*jien-yoo*

**syrup** 汤水 tangshui *tang-shweh*

**table** 桌子 zhuozi *jwo-ds*

**table cloth** 桌布 zhuobu
*jwo-boo*

**tablespoon** 勺子 shaozi
*shao-ds*, 汤匙 tangchi
*tang-chr*

**take, to** 把 ba *ba*

**talcum powder** 扑粉 pufen
*poo-fen*

**taste** 味 wei *way*; **taste, to**
尝 chang *chang*

**tasty** 好吃 haochi
*hao-chr*; 味道好
weidaohao *way-dao-hao*

**tea** 茶 cha *cha*; **jasmine tea**
花茶 huacha *hwa-cha*;
**black tea** 红茶 hongcha

*hong-cha*; **green tea** 绿茶
lücha *loo-cha*

**tea room** 茶馆 chaguan
*cha-gwan*

**teabag** 袋茶 daicha *dai-cha*

**teapot** 茶壶 chahu *cha-hoo*

**teaspoon** 小勺 xiaoshao
*siao-shao*

**telephone** 电话 dianhua
*dien-hwa*; **telephone, to**
打电话 da dianhua *da
dien-hwa*

**telephone directory**
电话本 dianhuaben
*dien-hwa-ben*

**temperature** 温度 wendu
*wen-doo*

**tender** 软 ruan *rwan*,
嫩 nen *nen*

**terminus** 终点站
zhongdianzhan
*joong-dien-jan*

**terrace** 阳台 yangtai
*yang-tai*

**thank you** 谢谢 xiexie
*sie-sie*

**that** 那个 nage *na-g*

**there isn't any, there
aren't any** 没有 meiyou

*may-yo*

**thin** 细 xi *see,* 薄 bo *boh;*
**thin lengths of pasta** 切面
qiemian *chie-mien;* **thin
slice** 片 pian *pien;* **thin
strip** 丝 si *s*

**thirst** 渴 ke *ke;* **I am thirsty**
我渴了 wo kele *woh ke-l*

**this** 这个 zhege *je-g*

**thread** 线 xian *sien*

**ticket** 票 piao *piao*

**time** 小时 xiaoshi *siao-shr*

**timetable** 时刻表
shikebiao *shr-ke-biao*

**tip** 小费 xiaofei *siao-fay*

**toast** 干杯 ganbei *gan-bay;*
**toast, to** 干杯 ganbei
*gan-bay;* **toasted bread**
烤面包 kaomianbao *kao-
mien-bao*

**toilet** 洗手间 xishoujian
*see-sho-jien,*厕所 cesuo
*ts-swo*

**tofu** 豆腐 doufu *toe-foo*

**tomato** 西红柿 xihongshi
*see-hong-shr*

**tongue** 舌头 shetou *shr-toe*

**too** 也 ye *yeh*

**too much** 太多 taiduo

*dai-dwo*

**toothpicks** 牙签 yaqian
*ya-chien*

**towel** 毛巾 maojin *mao-jin*

**town** 城市 chengshi
*cheng-shr*

**train** 火车 huoche *hwo-che*

**transport** 运输 yunshu
*yun-shoo*

**traveler's check** 旅行支票
luxing zhipiao *loo-sing
jr-piao*

**tray** 托盘 tuopan *two-pan*

**tripe** 肚 du *doo*

**trout** 鳟鱼 zunyu *dsoon-yoo*

**truffle** 香菇 xianggu
*siang-goo*

**tuna fish** 金浅鱼
jinqianyu *jin-chien-yoo*

**turkey** 火鸡 huoji *hwo-jee*

**turn off, to** 关 guan *gwan;*
关上 guanshang *gwan-shan*

**turn on, to** 点灯
diandeng *dien-deng*

**turnip** 萝 luobo *lwo-boh*

**turtle** 乌龟 wugui
*woo-gweh*

**try, to** 试 shi *shr,* 尝
chang *chang*

**uncomfortable** 不方便 bufangbian *boo-fang-bien*

**under** 下边 xiabian *sia-bien*

**under cover** 屋内 wunei *woo-nay*,里面 limian *lee-mien*

**understand, to** 明白 mingbai *ming-bai*, 懂 dong *dong*

**United States** 美国 Meiguo *may-gwo*

**utensil** 工具 gongju *goong-joo*

**vacation** 假日 jiari *jia-r*, 节日 jieri *jie-r*

**veal** 小牛 xiaoniu *siao-niu*

**vegetables** 豆子 douzi *doe-ds*; 蔬菜 shucai *shoo-tsai*; 蔬菜 qingcai *ching-tsai*

**vegetarian** 吃素者 chisuzhe *chr-soo-j*

**vermouth** 味美思 weimeisi *way-may-s*

**vinegar** 醋 cu *tsoo*

**vitamins** 维生素 weishengsu *way-sheng-soo*

**vodka** 俄得克 edeke *e-d-ke*

**wafer** 夹馅饼干 jiaxian binggan *jia-sien bing-gan*

**wait, to** 等 deng *deng*

**waiter/waitress** 服务员 fuwuyuan *foo-woo-ywen*

**wallet** 钱包 qianbao *chien-bao*

**want, to** 喜欢 xihuan *see-hwan*;要 yao *yao*

**warn, to** 告诉 gaosu *gao-soo*

**wash, to** 洗 xi *see*

**water** 水 shui *shweh*; **boiled water** 开水 kaishui *kai-shweh*; **water that is boiled and cooled** 谅开水 liangkaishui *liang-kai-shweh*, 冰水 bingshui *bing-shweh*; **sparkling water** 呆气水 daiqi shui *dai-chee shweh*; **mineral water** 矿泉水 kuangquanshui *kwang-chooan-shweh*; **still water** 不呆气水 bu daiqi shui *boo-dai-chee shweh*

**water chestnut** 栗子
lizi *lee-ds*

**watermelon** 西瓜 xigua
*see-gwa*

**week** 星期 xingqi
*sing-chee*

**welcome** 欢饮 huanying
*hwan-ying*

**what, which** 哪个 nage
*na-g*

**wheat** 大麦 damai *da-mai*

**when** 什么时候 shenme
shihou *scen-m shr-ho*

**where?** 什么地方 shenme
difang? *shem-moh
dee-fang*; 在哪儿 zai nar?
*dsai-nar?*

**whichever** 任何 renhe
*ren-heh*

**whisk, to** 搅打 jiaoda
*jiao-da*

**whisky** 威士忌 weishiji
*way-shr-jee*

**white** 白 bai *bai*

**white coffee** 牛奶咖啡
niunai kafei *niu-nai
ka-fay*

**wholemeal** 全麦面
quanmaimian *chwen-*

*mai-mien*

**window** 窗户 chuanghu
*chwang-hoo*

**wine** (grape) 葡萄酒
putaojiu *poo-tao-jioh*;
**white wine** 白葡萄酒
bai putaojiu *bai
poo-tao-jioh*; **rice wine**
米酒 mijiu *mee-jioh*; **rosé
wine** 玫瑰红酒
meiguihong jiu *may-
gweh-hong jioh*; **red
wine** 红葡萄酒 hong
putaojiu *hong poo-tao-jioh*

**without** 没有 meiyou
*may-yo*

**wok** 锅 guo *gwo*

**work (function), to** 行 xing
*sing*

**write, to** 写 xie *sie*

**year** 年 nian *nien*

**yeast** 酵母 jiaomu
*jiao-moo*

**yellow** 黄 huang *hwang*

**yogurt** 酸牛奶 suanniunai
*swan-niu-nai*

**young lady** 小姐 xiaojie
*siao-jie*

171

**anchun** 鹌鹑 *an-choon*
quail
**anjing** 安静 *an-jing* calm

**ba** 把 *ba* to take
**babao daya** 八宝大鸭
*ba-bao da-ya*, see
Regional dishes, p. 63
**babao fan** 八宝饭 *ba-bao
fan*, see National dishes,
p. 50
**bagua tang** 八卦汤 *ba-
gwa tang*, see Cuisine
and medicine, p. 36
**bai** 白 *bai* white
**bai putaojiu** 白葡萄酒
*bai poo-tao-jioh* white
wine
**baicai** 白菜 *bai-tsai*
Chinese cabbage, see
Condiments and main
ingredients, p. 27
**baihehua** 百合花 *bai-heh-
hwa* lily flowers, see
Condiments and main
ingredients, p. 27
**baijiu** 白酒 *bai-jioh*
liqueur, see Gastronomic
terms, p. 96
**bailandi** 白兰地 *bai-lan-*

*dee* grappa
**bainian jidan** 百年鸡蛋
*bai-nien jee-dan* eggs of
the 100 years, see
National dishes, p. 50
**baishi kele** 白事可乐
*bai-shr ke-le* Pepsi-Cola
**baishu** 白薯 *bai-shoo*
sweet potato
**bajiao** 八角 *ba-jiao*
aniseed, see Condiments
and main ingredients, p.
26
**Bali** 巴黎 *ba-lee* Paris
**bangzhu** 帮助 *bang-joo* to
help
**banshudan** 半熟蛋 *ban-
shoo-dan* boiled egg
**bao** 炮 *bao*, see
Gastronomic terms, p. 96
**bao bing** 薄饼 *bao bing*,
see Beijing kaoya,
Regional dishes, p. 59
**baohuji** 保护剂 *bao-
hoo-jee* preservative
**baokuo** 包括 *bao-kwo*
included
**baozi** 包子 *bao-ds*
steamed filled bread, see
Dim sum, p. 38

**basi** 拔丝 *ba-s* caramelized, see Gastronomic terms, p. 96

**basi shuiguo** 拔丝水果 *ba-s shweh-gwo* fruit that is fried and caramelized, see Regional dishes, p. 66 and Recipes, p. 75

**bei** 杯 *bay* little cup

**Beijing** 北京 *bay-jing* Beijing

**Beijing kaoya** 北京烤鸭 *bay-jing kao-ya* Beijing crispy duck, see Regional dishes, p. 59

**Beijing tezhong pijiu** 北京特种啤酒 *bay-jing te-joong pee-jioh* special Beijing beer, see Beverages, p. 25

**beimuji** 贝母鸡 *bay-moo-jee* pheasant

**beizi** 杯子 *bay-ds* glass

**benfangde** 本方的 *ben-fang-d* local

**biancan** 便餐 *bien-tsan* fixed-price menu

**biandou** 扁豆 *bien-doe* string bean

**bianhua** 变化 *bien-hwa* to change

**bianyi** 便宜 *bien-ee* cheap

**biaoshi** 表示 *biao-shr* to show

**bing** 冰 *bing* ice

**bing** 饼 *bing*, see Gastronomic terms, p. 96

**binggan** 饼干 *bing-gan* biscuit

**binggunr** 冰棍 *bing-goor* ice-lolly

**bingkuair** 冰块儿 *bing-kwair* ice cube

**bingqiling** 冰淇淋 *bing-chee-ling* ice-cream

**bingqilingdian** 冰淇淋店 *bing-chee-ling-dien* ice-cream parlor

**bingshui** 冰水 *bing-shweh* water that is boiled and cooled, see Beverages, p. 12

**bingtang hulu** 冰糖葫芦 *bing-tang hoo-loo*, see Dim sum, p. 38

**bingxiang** 冰箱 *bing-siang* refrigerator

**bixuzuode** 必须作的 *bee-soo-dswo-d* compulsory

**bo** 薄 *boh* fine

**bocai** 菠菜 *boh-tsai* spinach

**bocaiban fensi** 薄菜般
粉丝 *boh-tsai-ban fen-s*,
see National dishes, p. 50

**bohe** 薄荷 *boh-heh* mint

**boluo** 菠萝 *boh-lwo* pineapple

**bopi** 剥皮 *boh-pee* to peel

**bowuguan** 博物馆 *boh-
woo-gwan* museum

**bu** 不 *boo* no, not

**bu daiqi shui** 不呆气水
*boo dai-chee shweh*
natural water

**buding** 布丁 *boo-ding*
pudding

**buduo** 不多 *boo-dwo*
little

**bufangbian** 不方便 *boo-
fang-bien* uncomfortable

**buhan jiujingde** 不含酒
精的 *boo-han jioh-jing-d*
nonalcoholic

**buhan jiujing de yinliao**
不含酒精的饮料 *boo-
han jioh-jing-d yin-liao*
soft drink

**buhao** 不好 *boo-hao*
bad

**buxing** 不行 *boo-sing* out

of order

**cai** 菜 *tsai* dish; course

**caidan** 菜单 *tsai-dan*
menu

**caigua** 菜瓜 *tsai-gwa*
zucchini

**caihua** 菜花 *tsai-hwa*
cauliflower

**candou** 蚕豆 *tsan-doe*
broad beans

**canjin** 餐巾 *tsan-jin*
napkin

**canju** 餐具 *tsan-joo* cutlery

**canting** 餐厅 *tsan-ting*
restaurant

**caogu laochou** 草菇老抽
*tsao-goo lao-cho* soy
sauce with mushrooms,
see Condiments and main
ingredients, p. 32

**caomei** 草莓 *tsao-may*
strawberry

**cesuo** 厕所 *ts-swo* toilet

**cha** 茶 *cha* tea; infusion,
see Beverages, p. 13

**chabuduo** 差不多 *cha-
boo-dwo* almost

**chaguan** 茶馆 *cha-gwan*
tea room

**chahu** 茶壶 *cha-hoo* teapot

**chang** 尝 *chang* to taste

**Changchen** 长城 *chang-chen*, see Beverages, p. 24; Great Wall

**changshao** 长勺 *chang-shao* ladle

**chao** 吵 *chao* noise

**chao** 炒 *chao* to stir-fry, see Cooking methods, p. 49 and Gastronomic terms, p. 96

**chao doujiao** 炒豆角 *chao doe-jiao*, see National dishes, p. 50

**chao jielan** 炒芥兰 *chao jie-lan*, see Regional dishes, p. 64

**chao hundun** 炒馄饨 *chao hoon-doon* fried wonton, see Dim sum, p. 38

**chao shucai** 炒蔬菜 *chao shoo-tsai* stir-fried vegetables, see National dishes, p. 51 and Recipes, p. 76

**chaoji shichang** 超级市场 *chao-jee shr-chang* supermarket

**chao sishu** 炒四蔬 *chao s-shoo*, see National dishes, p. 51

**chaodan** 炒蛋 *chao-dan* scrambled egg

**chaode** 吵的 *chao-d* noisy

**chaomian** 炒面 *chao-mien* fried noodles

**chashao** 叉烧 *cheea-shao*, see Cooking methods, p. 49 and Regional dishes, p. 64

**chazi** 叉子 *cha-ds* fork

**chengshi** 城市 *cheng-shr* town, city

**chenpi** 陈皮 *chen-pee* see Gastronomic terms, p. 96

**chenpi niurou** 陈皮牛肉 *chen-pee neeoo-ro*, see Regional dishes, p. 69

**chenzi** 橙子 *chen-ds* orange

**chezhan** 车站 *che-jan* station

**chifan** 吃饭 *chr-fan* to eat

**chisuzhe** 吃素着 *chr-soo-j* vegetarian (noun)

**chisude** 吃素的 *chr-soo-d* vegetarian (adj.)

**choudoufu** 臭豆腐 *cho-toefoo* fermented tofu,

see Condiments and main ingredients, p. 33

**chuan** 串 *chwan* spit-roasted, skewer, see Gastronomic terms, p. 96

**chuanghu** 窗户 *chwan-hoo* window

**chuanyangrou tang** 川羊肉汤 *chwan-yang-ro tang*, see Regional dishes, p. 59

**chufang** 厨房 *choo-fang* kitchen

**chuke** 除壳 *choo-ke* to shell

**chukou** 出口 *choo-ko* exit, way out

**chulai** 出来 *choo-lai* to go out

**chunhuangju** 春黄菊 *choon-hwang-joo* camomile

**chuncong** 春葱 *choon-tsong* spring onion, see Condiments and main ingredients, p. 27

**chunjuan** 春卷 *choon-jwan* spring roll, see Dim sum, p. 38 and Recipes, p. 77

**chuqu** 出去 *choo-choo* to go out

**chuqu kafeiyinde** 除去咖

啡因的 *choo-choo kafay-yin-d* decaffeinated coffee

**chushi** 厨师 *choo-shr* cook

**chuzu** 出租 *choo-dsoo* hire

**cong** 葱 *tsong* onion

**congtou chao niurou** 葱头炒牛肉 *tsong-toe chao neeoo-ro*, see National dishes, p. 51

**congyou bing** 葱油饼 *tsong-yo bing*, see Regional dishes, p. 60

**cu** 醋 *tsoo* vinegar, see Condiments and main ingredients, p. 26

**cui** 脆 *tsweh* crisp

**da** 大 *da* big, large

**da dianhua** 打电话 *da dien-hwa* to telephone

**dacong** 大葱 *da-tsong* leek

**dadou** 大豆 *da-doe* soya

**daicha** 袋茶 *dai-cha* tea bag

**daiqi** 呆气 *dai-chee* fizzy

**daiqishui** 呆气水 *dai-chee-shweh* sparkling water

**daiqi yinliao** 呆气饮料 *dai-chee yin-liao* fizzy

drink

**dajiao** 大椒 *da-jiao* pepper

**dakai** 打开 *da-kai* to open

**damai** 大麦 *da-mai* corn, barley

**dami** 大米 *da-mee*, rice see Condiments and main ingredients, p. 30

**dancai** 淡菜 *dan-tsai* mussels

**dandan mian** 旦旦面 *dan-dan mien* dandan noodles, see National dishes, p. 51, and Recipes, p. 79

**dangao** 蛋糕 *dan-gao* soft sweet (similar to sponge cake)

**danhuang** 蛋黄 *dan-hwang* egg yolk

**dansu baozi** 蛋素包子 *dan-soo bao-ds*, see Dim sum, p. 38

**danqing** 蛋清 *dan-ching* egg white

**daocha** 刀叉 *dao-cha* cutlery

**daoda** 到达 *dao-da* to arrive

**daozi** 刀子 *dao-ds* knife

**daren** 大人 *da-ren* adult

**dashiguan** 大使馆 *da-shr-gwan* embassy

**dasuan** 大蒜 *da-swan* garlic

**dasuan kongxincai** 大蒜空心菜 *da-swan koong-sin-tsai*, see Regional dishes, p. 69

**dating** 大厅 *da-ting* room

**daxia** 大虾 *da-sia* prawn

**deng** 灯 *deng* lamp

**deng** 等 *deng* to wait

**deng** 登 *deng* to go up

**dian** 店 *dien* premises, shop

**diandeng** 点灯 *dien-deng* to turn on the light

**dianhuaben** 电话本 *dien-hwa-ben* telephone directory

**dianti** 电梯 *dien-tee* elevator

**dianxin** 点心 *dien-sin* snack, see Dim sum, p. 37 and Gastronomic terms, p. 96

**diaoyu** 鲷渔 *diao-yoo* sea bream

**difang** 地方 *dee-fang* place

**dianhua** 电话 *dien-hwa*
telephone

**diaoyu** 钓鱼 *diao-yoo*
fish, to fish

**ding** 丁 *ding*, see
Gastronomic terms, p. 97

**ding** 定 *ding* to order, to
reserve, reservation

**dingjin** 定金 *ding-jin*
depot

**dingxiang** 丁香 *ding-siang*
cloves

**dingzuo** 定做 *ding-dswo*
to order/to reserve

**dizhi** 地址 *dee-j* address

**dong** 懂 *dong* to understand

**dongchong kaoya** 冬虫烤
鸭 *doong-chong kao-ya*, see
Cuisine and medicine, p. 36

**dongjiang yanjiu ji** 东江
盐酒鸡 *doong-jiang yan-
jeeoo jee*, see Reg. dishes, p. 64

**dou** 都 *doe* all

**doufu** 豆腐 *toe-foo*
tofu see Condiments
and main ingredients,
p. 33

**doufugan** 豆腐干 *toefoo-
gan* dried tofu, see
Condiments and main

ingredients, p. 33

**doufunao** 豆腐脑
*toefoo-nao* tofu-brain, see
Condiments and main
ingredients, p. 33

**doufuru** 豆腐 *toefoo-roo*
fermented tofu, see
Condiments and main
ingredients, p. 33

**doufu xiaren tang** 豆腐虾
仁汤 *toefoo sia-ren tang*,
see National dishes, p. 51

**doujiao** 豆角 *doe-jiao*
sweet-pea

**doukou** 豆蔻 *doe-ko*
nutmeg

**doupi** 豆皮 *doe-pee*
pod

**douya** 豆芽 *doe-ya*
beansprouts, see
Condiments and main
ingredients, p. 28

**douzi** 豆子 *doe-ds* bean,
pulse

**du** 肚 *doo* tripe

**dun** 炖 *doon* stewed,
see Gastronomic terms,
p. 97

**duoshao** 多少 *dwo-shao*
how much, how many

**dusongzijiu** 杜松子酒
*doo-soong-ds-jioh* gin

**e** 饿  *e* hunger
**e** 鹅  *e* goose
**edeke** 俄得克 *e-d-ke*
vodka

**Faguo** 法国 *fa-gwo* France
**faguo bailandi** 法国白兰
地 *fa-gwo bai-lan-dee*
cognac
**faguoren** 法国人
*fa-gwo-ren* native of
France
**famianbing** 发面饼 *fa-mien-bing* leavened bread
**fan** 饭 *fan* food
**fandian** 饭店 *fan-dien*
hotel
**fangcao** 芳草 *fang-tsao*
aromatic herbs
**fangjian** 房间 *fang-jien*
room
**fanguan** 饭馆 *fan-gwan*
restaurant
**fangxian** 方向 *fang-sian*
direction
**fanhonghua** 番红花
*fan-hong-hwa* saffron

**fanpu** 饭铺 *fan-poo* cheap
restaurant
**fanqie danhua tang** 番茄
蛋花汤 *fan-chie dan-hwa
tang*, see National dishes,
p. 51
**fanshi** 饭食 *fan-shr* meal
**fanting** 饭厅 *fan-ting*
dining room
**fanzhuang** 饭庄 *fan-jwang*
restaurant
**fapiao** 发票 *fa-piao*
receipt
**fayu** 法语 *fa-yoo* French
(language)
**fei** 肥 *fay* fat
**fei** 飞 *fay* flight
**feizao** 肥皂 *fay-dsao* soap
**feicui fan** 翡翠饭 *fay-tsweh fan*, see Regional
dishes, p. 60
**feichang haochi** 非常好
吃 *fay-chang hao-ch* delicious
**feiji** 飞机 *fay-jee* airplane
**feijichang** 飞机场 *fay-jee-chang* airport
**feili** 非礼 *fay-lee* red mullet
**feiyu** 鲱渔 *fay-yoo* herring
**fen** 份 *fen* portion
**fengmi** 蜂蜜 *feng-mee* honey

**fenjiu** 汾酒 *fen-jioh*, see Beverages, p. 20

**fengzhong** 分钟 *feng-joong* minute

**fukuan** 付款 *foo-kwan* to pay, payment

**futuanzi** 浮团子 *foo-twan-ds*, see Yuanxiao, in Dim sum, p. 41

**fuwu** 服务 *foo-woo* service

**fuwuyuan** 服务员 *foo-woo-ywen* aiter/waitress

**gaibian** 改变 *gai-bien* to change

**gali** 咖哩 *ga-lee* curry

**gan** 肝 *gan* liver

**gan** 干 *gan* dry

**gan mogu** 干蘑菇 *gan moh-goo* dried mushrooms

**gan shuiguo** 干水果 *gan shweh-gwo* dried fruit

**ganbei** 干杯 *gan-bay* to drink to/toast, toast; cheers, your health

**gancao** 甘草 *gan-tsao* liquorice

**ganjing** 干净 *gan-jing* clean

**ganlan** 甘蓝 *gan-lan* olive

**ganlao** 干酪 *gan-lao* cheese

**ganzao** 干燥 *gan-tsao* dry

**ganju** 柑橘 *gan-joo* citrus

**ganzhu shuiguo** 柑橘水果 *gan-joo shweh-gwo* citrus fruit

**gaobing** 糕饼 *gao-bing* cake

**gaodian** 糕点 *gao-dien* sweet

**gaodiandian** 糕点店 *gao-dien-dien* patisserie

**gaojiaoyi** 高教椅 *gao-jiao-ee* highchair

**gaoliang** 高粱 *gao-liang* sorghum

**gaoliangjiu** 高粱酒 *gao-liang-jioh*, see Beverages, p. 20

**gaosu** 告诉 *gao-soo* to warn

**geng** 羹 *geng* soup

**geng xihuan** 更喜欢 *geng see-hwan* to prefer

**gezi** 鸽子 *ge-ds* pigeon

**gongbao jiding** 宫保鸡丁 *goong-bao jee-ding* chicken of the deputy king, see National dishes, p. 52, and Recipes, p. 80

**gonggong qiche** 公共汽车 *goong-goong chee-che* bus

**gongju** 工具 *goong-joo* utensil, implement

**gouqizi** 枸杞子 *go-chee-ds* lychee

**gouyu** 狗鱼 *go-yoo* pike

**gu** 骨 *goo* bone

**guaiwei** 怪味 *gwai-way*, see Gastronomic terms, p. 97

**guan** 关 *gwan* closed; to turn off

**guandijiu** 馆帝酒 *gwan-dee-jioh*, see Beverages, p. 21

**Guangdong chaofan** 广东炒饭 *gwang-doong chao-fan* Cantonese stir-fried rice, see Regional dishes, p. 64, and Recipes, p. 81

**guanli** 管理 *gwan-lee* mandarin (official)

**guanlichu** 管理处 *gwan-lee-choo* management

**guanmen** 关门 *gwan-men* to close, to shut

**guantourou** 罐头肉 *gwan-toe-ro* canned meat

**Guangzhou** 广州 *gwang-jo* Canton

**gui** 贵 *gwch* expensive

**guihua** 桂花 *gweh-hwa* osmanthus

**guihuajiu** 桂花酒 *gweh-hwa-jioh*, see Beverages, p. 23

**guipi** 桂皮 *gweh-pee* cinnamon

**guiyu** 鲑渔 *gweh-yoo* salmon

**gujinggon jiu** 古井贡酒 *goo-jing-goon jioh*, see Beverages, p. 21

**guke** 顾客 *goo-ke* client

**gulao rou** 古老肉 *goo-lao ro* sweet and sour pork, see National dishes, p. 52 and Recipes, p. 82

**guo** 锅 *gwo* wok; Chinese frying pan, see Cooking methods, p. 47

**guoba** 锅巴 *gwo-ba* fried rice, see Gastronomic terms, p. 97

**guodong** 果冻 *gwo-doong* gelatine

**guodongde** 果冻的 *gwo-doong-d* gelatinous

**guojia** 国家 *gwo-jia* nation

**guojiang** 果酱 *gwo-jiang* jam

**guojiang dangao** 果酱蛋糕 *gwo-jiang dan-gao*

pie

**guomin** 过敏 *gwo-min* allergy

**guorenr** 果仁儿 *gwo-ren* stone

**guotie jiao** 锅贴饺 *gwo-tieh jiao* stir-fried ravioli, see Dim sum, p. 39

**guozhi** 果汁 *gwo-j* fruit juice

**guzhang** 故障 *goo-jang* out of order

**hai** 还 *hai* again (adverb)

**hai** 海 *hai* sea

**haibian** 海边 *hai-bien* sea

**haixian** 海鲜 *hai-sien* seafood

**haixianjiang** 海鲜酱 *-sien-jiang* Hoisin sauce, see Condiments and main ingredients, p. 32

**haizi** 孩子 *hai-ds* child

**hangban** 航班 *hang-ban* flight

**hanjiujing** 含酒精 *han-jioh-jing* alcoholic

**hanyu** 汉语 *han-yoo* Chinese language

**hanzi** 汉字 *han-ds* Chinese characters

**hao** 好 *hao* well, good

**hao** 号 *hao* number

**hao** 蚝 *hao* oyster

**haochi** 好吃 *hao-chee* good (to eat)

**haoma** 号码 *hao-ma* number

**haoxiaohua** 好消化 *hao-siao-hwa* digestible

**haoyou** 蚝油 *hao-yo* oyster sauce, see Condiments and main ingredients, p. 31

**haoyou niurou** 好油牛肉 *hao-yo neeoo-ro*, see National dishes, p. 52

**he** 喝 *heh* to drink

**hebaodan** 荷包蛋 *heh-bao-dan* fried eggs

**heiculi** 黑醋栗 *hay-tsoo-lee* currant

**heikafei** 黑咖啡 *hay-ca-fay* black coffee

**heixianxue** 黑线鳕 *hay-sien-sweh* hake

**hetao** 核桃 *heh-tao* nut

**hetaojia** 核桃夹 *heh-tao-jia* nutcracker

**heye** 荷叶 *heh-yeh* lotus leaves, see Condiments and main ingredients, p. 27

**heye fenzheng niurou** 荷叶粉蒸牛肉 *heh-yeh fen-jeng neeoo-ro*, see Regional dishes, p. 69

**heye fengzheng rou** 荷叶粉蒸肉 *heh-yeh feng-jeng ro*, see Regional dishes, p. 66

**heye zhengyu** 荷叶蒸渔 *heh-yeh jeng-yoo*, see Regional dishes, p. 64

**hong** 红 *hong* red

**hong putaojiu** 红葡萄酒 *hong poo-tao-jioh* red wine

**hongcha** 红茶 *hong-cha* black tea, see Beverages, p. 15

**hongdou sha** 红豆沙 *hong-doe sha* sweet bean sauce, see Condiments and main ingredients, p. 30

**hongluobo** 红萝卜 *hong-lwo-boh* carrot

**hongshao** 红烧 *hong-shao*, see Gastronomic terms, p. 97

**hongshao yu** 红烧渔 *hong-shao yoo* braised fish in sweet and sour sauce, see National dishes, p. 52, and Recipes, p. 84

**hongyou** 红油 *hong-yo* red sauce, see Condiments and main ingredients, p. 32

**hongyou shuijiao** 红油水饺 *hong-yo shweh-jiao*, see Dim sum, p. 39

**houbi** 货币 *ho-bee* currency

**houyan** 火焰 *ho-yen* flame

**hu** 沪 *hoo* oven

**huacha** 花茶 *hwa-cha* aromatic tea, see Beverages, p. 16

**huai** 坏 *hwai* bad

**huajiao** 花椒 *hwa-jiao* Sichuan pepper, see Condiments and main ingredients, p. 29

**huan** 换 *hwan* to change (currency)

**huang** 黄 *hwang* yellow

**huangdi** 皇帝 *hwang-dee* emperor

**huanggua** 黄瓜 *hwang-gwa* cucumber

**Huanghe liyu** 黄河鲤鱼 *hwang-heh lee-yoo*, see Regional dishes, p. 60

**huanghelou jiu** 黄鹤楼酒 *hwang-heh-lo jioh*, see Beverages, p. 21

**huangjiu** 黄酒 *hwang-jioh*, see Beverages, p. 23

**huangyou** 黄油 *hwang-yo* butter

**huanying** 欢迎 *hwan-ying* welcome

**huaqishen dongchongcao dun ruge** 花旗参冬虫草炖乳鸽 *hwa-chee-shen doong-choong-tsao doon roo-ge*, see Cuisine and med., p. 36

**huasheng** 花生 *hwa-sheng* peanut

**huasheng you** 花生油 *hwa-sheng yo* peanut oil, see Condiments and main ingredients, p. 29

**huayecai** 花椰菜 *hwa-yeh-tsai* broccoli

**hui** 茴 *hweh* anise

**huixiang** 茴香 *hweh-siang* fennel

**huiguo rou** 回锅肉 *hweh-gwo ro* pork that returns to the pan, see Regional dishes, p. 70

**hujiaofen** 胡椒粉 *hoo-jiao-fen* pepper

**hujiaomo** 胡椒磨 *hoo-jiao-moh* pepper grinder

**hundun** 馄饨 *hoon-doon* wonton

**hundun tang** 馄饨汤 *hoon-doon tang* wonton soup, see Dim sum, p. 39 and Recipes, p. 86

**hunhe** 混合 *hoon-heh* mixture

**hunyou** 荤油 *hoon-yo* lard

**huo** 火 *hwo* fire

**huocai daimao** 和菜戴帽 *hwo-tsai dai-mao*, see Regional dishes, p. 60

**huoche** 火车 *hwo-che* train

**huoche zhan** 火车站 *hwo-che jan* railroad station

**huoguo** 火锅 *hwo-gwo*, see Regional dishes, p. 70

**huoji** 火鸡 *hwo-jee* turkey

**huotui** 火腿 *hwo-tweh*

ham
**huwai** 户外 *hoo-wai*
outside, in the open air

**ji** 鸡 *jee* cockerel
**ji** 蓟 *jee* thistle
**ji** 挤 *jee* crowded
**jia** 家 *jia* family
**jia tiaowei** 加调味 *jia tiao-way* to flavor
**jiacai mianbao** 夹菜面包 *jia-tsai mien-bao* filled roll
**jian** 肩 *jien* shoulder
**jian** 煎 *jien* fried, see Gastronomic terms, p. 97
**jian danjuanr** 煎蛋卷 *jien dan-jwar* omelet
**jiancha** 检查 *jien-cha* to check
**jiangcong pangxie** 姜葱螃蟹 pa*jiang-tsong pang-sie*, see Regional dishes, p. 65
**jiandan** 简单 *jien-dan* simple
**jiang** 酱 *jiang* sauce
**jianguo** 煎锅 *jien-gwo* pan
**jiangyou** 酱油 *jiang-yo*

soy sauce, see Condiments and main ingredients, p. 31
**jiannanchun jiu** 剑南春酒 *jien-nan-choon jioh*, see Beverages, p. 21
**jianyu** 箭鱼 *jien-yoo* sword fish
**jiao** 嚼 *jiao* to chew
**jiao ren** 叫人 *jiao ren* to call
**jiaoda** 搅打 *jiao-da* to whisk
**jiaomu** 酵母 *jiao-moo* yeast
**jiaotang** 焦糖 *jiao-tang* caramel
**jiaoyan xia** 椒盐虾 *jiao-yen sia*, see Regional dishes, p. 67
**jiaoyou** 郊游 *jiao-yo* trip, excursion
**jiaozi** 饺子 *jiao-ds* filled "parcel"; steamed ravioli, see Dim sum, p. 39
**jiaqian** 价钱 *jia-chien* price
**jiare** 加热 *jia-re* to heat
**jiari** 假日 *jia-r* holiday
**jiaxian** 夹馅 *jia-sien* filled,

stuffed
**jiaxian binggan** 夹馅饼干
*jia-sien bing-gan* wafer
**jiayouzhan** 加油站
*jia-yo-jan* gas
station
**jidan** 鸡蛋 *jee-dan* egg
**jie** 饥饿 *jie* hunger
**jieri** 节日 *jie-r* holiday
**jiemo** 芥末 *jie-moh* mustard
**jiemu** 节目 *jie-moo*
performance, show
**jiezai** 结采 *jie-dsai* mustard
**jiezhi** 节制 *jie-j* diet
**jiezhi yinshi** 节制饮食
*jie-j yin-shr* diet
**jige** 几个 *jee-ge* how many, how much
**jingjiu** 京酒 *jing-jioh*,
see Beverages, p. 21
**jingli** 经理 *jing-lee* manager
**jinjiang rousi** 京酱肉丝
*jin-jiang ro-s*, see
Regional dishes, p. 60
**jinqiangyu** 金枪渔 *jin-chien-yoo* tuna fish
**jinxianyu** 金线玉 *jin-sien-yoo*, see Regional dishes, p. 70
**jin zhu** 金猪 *jin joo*
golden piglet, see
Regional dishes, p. 65

**jisi chaofan** 鸡丝炒饭
*jee-s chao-fan* stir-fried
rice with chicken, see
National dishes, p. 53
**jisi chaomian** 鸡丝炒面
*jee-s chao-mien* stir-fried
noodles with chicken, see
National dishes, p. 53
**jiu** 酒 *jioh* wine, liqueur,
see Beverages, p. 19
**jiuba** 酒吧 *jioh-ba* bar
**jiucai** 酒菜 *jioh-tsai*
appetizer, see
Gastronomic terms, p. 97
**jiudian** 酒店 *jioh-dien*
restaurant
**jiujing** 酒精 *jioh-jing*
alcoholic
**jizhou** 鸡粥 *jee-jo*, see
Dim sum, p. 39
**ji zhuo doufu** 鸡啄豆腐
*jee jwo toefoo*, see
National dishes, p. 53
**juan** 卷 *jwan* "parcel",
sheet of pastry
**juheguo** 聚合果 *joo-heh-gwo* berry
**juhua** 菊花 *joo-hwa*
chrysanthemum
**juhua rouwan** 菊花肉丸

*joo-hwa ro-wan*, see Regional dishes, p. 67

**juju** 菊苣 *joo-joo* chicory

**juju ji** 榉榉鸡 *joo-joo jee*, see Regional dishes, p. 71

**jumaicai** 苣荬菜 *joo-mai-tsai* endive

**juyuan** 枸橼 *joo-ywen* cedar

**juzhi** 桔汁 *joo-j* orange juice

**juzi** 桔子 *joo-ds* mandarin (fruit)

**juzishui** 桔子水 *joo-ds-shweh* orangeade

**kafei** 咖啡 *ka-fay* coffee

**kafeiguan** 咖啡馆 *ka-fay-gwan* café, bar

**kafeiyin** 咖啡因 *ka-fay-yin* caffeine

**kai shui** 开水 *kai shweh* water that is boiled and cooled, see Beverages, p. 12

**kaiguanqi** 开罐器 *kai-gwan-chee* can opener

**kaipingqi** 开瓶器 *kai-ping-chee* bottle opener

**kaiweijiu** 开胃酒 *kai-way-*

*jioh* appetizer

**kaixinguo** 开心果 *kai-sin-gwo* pistachio

**kaixiao** 开销 *kai-siao* shopping

**kaizhede** 开着的 *kai-j-de* open

**kaluli** 卡路里 *ka-loo-lee* calorie

**kanmenren** 看门人 *kan-men-ren* custodian

**kao** 烤 *kao* see Gastronomic terms, p. 97

**kaobing** 烤饼 *kao-bing* bread, "focaccia"

**kaode** 烤的 *kao-d* baked, roasted

**kaojia** 烤架 *kao-jia* grill

**kaojiade** 烤架的 *kao-jia-d* grilled

**kaomianbao** 烤面包 *kao-mien-bao* toast

**kaomianbing** 烤面饼 *kao-mien-bing* bread, "focaccia"

**kaopan** 烤盘 *kao-pan* pie-dish

**kaoqian** 烤钎 *kao-chien* spit

**kaoyadian** 烤鸭店 *kao-ya-dien* restaurant that serves crispy duck

**kapuqinuo kafei** 卡普契
诺咖啡 *ka-poo-chee-nwo ka-fay* cappuccino

**ke** 渴 *ke* thirst

**keke** 可可 *ke-ke* cocoa

**kekou kele** 可口可乐 *ke-ko ke-le* Coca-Cola

**kong** 空 *koong* empty

**kongqi** 空气 *koong-chee* air

**kongtiao** 空调 *koong-tiao* air conditioning

**Kongzi** 孔子 *koong-ds* Confucius

**kou** 口 *ko* mouth

**kouwei** 口味 *ko-way* aroma

**kouweide** 口味的 *ko-way-d* aromatic

**kouxiangtan** 蔻香糖 *ko-siang-tan* chewing gum

**ku** 苦 *koo* bitter

**kuai** 块 *kwai* slice

**kuai** 快 *kwai* fast

**kuaicandian** 快吃店 *kwai-tsan-dien* fast-food

**kuair** 块儿 *kwair* piece

**kuaizi** 筷子 *kwai-ds* chopsticks

**kuangquanshui** 矿泉水 *kwang-chwen-shweh* mineral water

**kuihua** 葵花 *kweh-hwa*, see Beverages, p. 24

**la** 辣 *la* spicy

**ladouban jiang** 辣豆瓣酱 *la-doe-ban jiang* spicy bean sauce, see Condiments and main ingredients, p. 31

**laidao** 来到 *lai-dao* to arrive

**lajiang** 辣酱 *la-jiang* spicy soy sauce, see Condiments and main ingredients, p. 32

**lajiao** 辣椒 *la-jiao* pepper, chili pepper

**lajiao you** 辣椒油 *la-jiao yo* chili oil, see Condiments and main ingredients, p. 28

**lao** 老 *lao* old

**laochou wang** 老抽王 *lao-cho wang* dark soy sauce, see Condiments and main ingredients, p. 31

**laojiuhan** 老酒汗 *lao-jioh-han*, see Beverages, p. 21

**leng** 冷 *leng* cold

**li** 梨 *lee* pear

**liangshi** 粮食 *liang-shr* cereals

**lianhua** 莲花 *lien-hwa* lotus

**liankaishui** 凉开水 *lien-kai-shweh* water that is boiled and cooled

**lianpeng** 莲蓬 *lien-peng* lotus roots

**lianzi** 莲子 *lien-ds* lotus seeds

**liji** 里脊 *lee-jee* fillet

**lijiu** 烈酒 *lee-jioh* spirit

**limian** 里面 *lee-mien* under cover

**lingdui** 领队 *ling-dweh* chaperon, group leader

**liyu** 鲤鱼 *lee-yoo* carp

**lizhi** 荔枝 *lee-jr* lychee

**lizi** 栗子 *lee-ds* water chestnut, see Condiments and main ingredients, p. 26

**lizi** 李子 *lee-ds* plum

**longxia** 龙虾 *long-sia* lobster

**lou** 楼 *lo* floor (of a building)

**lu** 绿 *loo* green

**lu** 鹿 *loo* deer

**lu** 路 *loo* road

**lu** 鲈 *loo* perch (fish)

**lücha** 绿茶 *loo-cha* green tea, see Beverages, p. 15

**Lundun** 伦敦 *loon-doon* London

**Luoma** 罗马 *lwo-ma* Rome

**luobo** 萝卜 *lwo-boh* horse-radish; radish, turnip

**luole** 罗勒 *lwo-le* basil

**lusun** 芦笋 *loo-soon* asparagus

**luxing zhipiao** 旅行支票 *loo-sing jr-piao* traveler's check

**luyu** 鲈渔 *loo-yoo* bass

**luzhou laojiao** 泸州老窖 *loo-joo lao-jiao*, see Beverages, p. 21

**mahua** 麻花 *ma-hwa*, see Dim sum, p. 40

**mai** 买 *mai* to buy

**mai** 卖 *mai* to sell

**mai dongxi** 买东西 *mai doong-see* to do the shopping

**majiang** 麻酱 *ma-jiang*

sesame sauce, see Condiments and main ingredients, p. 31

**majiang** 麻将 *ma-jiang* mahjong

**mala** 麻辣 *ma-la*, see Gastronomic terms, p. 98

**mala jiding** 麻辣鸡丁 *ma-la jee-ding*, see National dishes, p. 54

**malingshu** 马铃薯 *ma-ling-shoo* potato

**mang** 忙 *mang* engaged

**mangguo** 芒果 *mang-gwo* mango

**manli** 鳗鲡 *man-lee* eel

**manmandi** 漫漫地 *man-man-dee* slow, slowly

**mantou** 馒头 *man-toe* steamed bread, see Dim sum, p. 40

**maotaijiu** 茅台酒 *mao-tai-jioh* Maotai, see Beverages, p. 22

**mapo doufu** 麻婆豆腐 *ma-poh toefoo* tofu of the pock-marked old lady, see National dishes, p. 54 and Recipes, p. 88

**mayi shangshu** 蚂蚁上树 *ma-ee shang-shoo* ants that climb up the tree, see Regional dishes, p. 71

**meigui** 玫瑰 *may-gweh* rose (flower)

**meiguihong jiu** 玫瑰红酒 *may-gweh-hong jioh* rosé wine

**meiguilu** 玫瑰露 *may-gweh-loo*, see Beverages, p. 22

**Meiguo** 美国 *may-gwo* U.S.A.

**meiguoren** 美国人 *may-gwo-ren* American (native of the United States)

**meili** 美丽 *may-lee* beautiful

**meishude** 没熟的 *may-shoo-d* raw

**meiyou** 没有 *may-yo* there isn't any, there aren't any

**men** 门 *men* door

**mian** 面 *mien* noodles, see Condiments and main ingredients, p. 32

**mianbao** 面包 *mien-bao* sandwich bread

**mianfei** 免费 *mien-fay* free

**mianfen** 面粉 *mien-fen*

flour

**mianshi** 面食 *mien-shr* pasta

**miantiao** 面条 *mien-tiao* noodles

**mianzhi** 面纸 *mien-jr* napkin, paper handkerchief

**midiexiang** 迷迭香 *mee-die-siang* rosemary

**mifan** 米饭 *mee-fan* boiled rice, see National dishes, p. 54

**mifen** 米粉 *mee-fen* thin noodles, rice noodles; rice flour

**mihoutao** 猕猴桃 *mee-ho-tao* kiwi

**mijian** 密饯 *mee-jien* candies

**mijiu** 米酒 *mee-jioh* rice wine, see Beverages, p. 23

**mingbai** 明白 *ming-bai* to understand

**mingxinpian** 明信片 *ming-sin-pien* post card

**mingzi** 名字 *ming-ds* name

**mizao yangrou** 蜜枣羊肉 *mee-dsao yang-ro*, see Cuisine and medicine, p. 36

**modouyu** 墨斗渔 *moh-doe-yoo* cuttlefish

**mogu** 蘑菇 *moh-goo* mushroom, see Condiments and main ingredients, p. 27

**mogu caixin** 蘑菇菜心 *moh-goo tsai-sin*, see National dishes, p. 54

**molihua** 茉莉花 *moh-lee-hwa* jasmine

**mugua** 木瓜 *moo-gwa* papaya, papaw

**muji** 母鸡 *moo-jee* hen

**mulan** 木兰 *moo-lan* magnolia

**muxu rou** 木须肉 *moo-soo ro*, see National dishes, p. 54

**nage** 哪个 *na-g* what, which

**nage** 那个 *na-g* that

**naifen** 奶粉 *nai-fen* powdered milk

**nailo** 奶酪 *nai-loh* cheese

**naiyou** 奶油 *nai-yo* custard, cream

**nangua** 南瓜 *nan-gwa* pumpkin

**Nanjing** 南京 *nan-jing*
Nanchino

**Nanjing yanshuiya** 南京
盐水鸭 *nan-jing yen-shweh-ya*, see Regional dishes, p. 67

**naozi** 脑子 *nao-ds* brain

**neizang** 内脏 *nay-dsang*
entrails

**nen** 嫩 *nen* tender

**nian** 年 *nien* year

**nianmi** 黏米 *nien-mee*
glutinous rice

**niangzao** 酿造 *niang-dsao* to ferment

**ningmeng** 柠檬 *ning-meng* lemon

**ningmeng qishui** 柠檬汽
水 *ning-meng chee-shweh* lemonade

**niu** 牛 *niu* ox

**niunai** 牛奶 *niu-nai* milk

**niunai kafei** 牛奶咖啡
*niu-nai ca-fay* milky coffee

**niupai** 牛排 *niu-pai*
steak

**niurou** 牛肉 *niu-ro*
beef

**niurou chaofan** 牛肉炒饭
*niu-ro chao-fan* stir-fried rice with beef, see

National dishes, p. 54

**niurou chaomian** 牛肉炒
面 *niu-ro chao-mien* stir-fried noodles with beef, see National dishes, p. 55

**Niuyue** 纽约 *niu-yweh*
New York

**nuanqi** 纽约 *nwan-chee*
heating

**nushi** 暖气 *noo-shr* lady

**ou** 藕 *oe* lotus root

**ouqincai** 欧芹菜 *oe-chin-tsai* parsley

**oushicai** 欧莳菜 *oe-shr-tsai* cumin

**paigu** 排骨
*pai-goo* (large)
chop

**pangxie** 螃蟹 *pang-sie*
crab

**panzi** 盘子 *pan-ds* dish

**paocai** 泡菜 *pao-tsai*
pickles

**pengren** 烹饪 *peng-ren*
gastronomy

**pengtiao** 烹调 *peng-tiao*
culinary art, see Cooking methods, p. 47

**pengtiaofa** 烹调法 *peng-tiao-fa* recipe

**pengyou** 朋友 *peng-yo* friend

**pi** 皮 *pee* peel

**pian** 片 *pien*, see Gastronomic terms, p. 98

**piao** 票 *piao* ticket

**piaoliang** 漂亮 *piao-liang* beautiful

**pijiu** 啤酒 *pee-jioh* beer, see Beverages, p. 25

**ping** 瓶 *ping* bottle

**pingguo** 苹果 *ping-gwo* apple

**pingjing** 平静 *ping-jing* calm

**pingsai** 瓶塞 *ping-sai* cork, stopper

**pingyu** 平鱼 *ping-yoo* sole

**pingzhuang** 平装 *ping-jooang* bottled

**pinpan** 拼盘 *pin-pan* cold sliced meat; appetizer

**pinyin** 拼音 *pin-yin* system of transcribing Chinese pronunciation, see Note on pronunciation, p. 3

**pipa** 皮杷 *pee-pa* medlar

**pufen** 扑粉 *poo-fen* talcum powder

**putao** 葡萄 *poo-tao* grapes

**putaogan** 葡萄干 *poo-tao-gan* raisin

**putaojiu** 葡萄酒 *poo-tao-jioh* wine

**putonghua** 普通话 *poo-tong-hwa* Chinese mandarin

**qianbao** 钱包 *chien-bao* wallet

**qiang huanggua** 炝黄瓜 *chiang hwang-gwa*, see National dishes, p. 55

**qianming** 签名 *chien-ming* signature

**qiaokeli** 巧克力 *chiao-ke-lee* chocolate

**qie** 切 *chie* to cut, mince

**qiemian** 切面 *chie-mien* long (thin) strips of pasta

**qiezi** 茄子 *chie-ds* eggplant

**qijiu** 汽酒 *chee-jioh* sparkling wine

**qincai** 芹菜 *chin-tsai* celery

**qing** 请 *ching* to invite

**qing** 轻 *ching* light

**qingcai** 青菜 *ching-tsai* vegetable

**qingkejiu** 青稞酒 *ching-*

*ke-jioh*, see Beverages, p. 22

**qingwa** 青蛙 *ching-wa* frog

**qingtang** 清汤 *ching-tang* broth

**qishui** 汽水 *chee-shweh* fizzy drink

**qita** 其他 *chee-ta* other

**quanmaimian** 全麦面 *chwen-mai-mien* wholemeal

**quanxing daqu** 全兴大曲 *chwen-sing da-choo*, see Beverages, p. 22

**queren** 确认 *chweh-ren* to confirm

**quxiao** 取消 *choo-siao* to cancel

**ranshao** 燃烧 *ran-shao* burned

**re** 热 *re* hot

**renhe** 任何 *ren-heh* any

**renshen** 人参 *ren-shen* jinseng

**rou** 肉 *ro* meat, pulp

**rougui** 肉桂 *ro-gweh* laurel

**roushang** 肉商 *ro-shang* butcher

**roushi** 肉食 *ro-shr* sausage

**rousong** 肉松 *ro-soong* minced meat

**routang** 肉汤 *ro-tang* meat broth

**ruan** 软 *rwan* tender

**ruanti dongwu** 软体动物 *rwan-tee dong-woo* mollusk

**ruanyinliao** 软饮料 *rwan-yin-liao* nonalcoholic

**rukou** 入口 *roo-ko* entrance

**ruzhipin** 乳制品 *roo-jr-pin* dairy products

**shadingyu** 沙丁渔 *sha-ding-yoo* sardine

**shaguo** 沙锅 *sha-gwo* saucepan

**shaguo doufu** 沙锅豆腐 *sha-gwo toefoo*, see National dishes, p. 55

**shala** 沙拉 *sha-la* lettuce

**shanbei** 扇贝 *shan-bay* coquilles St. Jacques

**Shandong ya** 山东鸭 *shan-doong ya*, see Regional dishes, p. 61

**shang** 上 *shang* to go up

**shangbian** 上边 *shang-bien* above

**Shanghai** 上海 *shang-hai*
Shanghai

**Shanghai tezhong pijiu**
上海特种啤酒 *shang-hai
te-joong pee-jioh* special
Shanghai beer, see
Beverages, p. 25

**shanhu baicai** 珊瑚白菜
*shan-hoo bai-tsai*, see
Regional dishes, p. 67

**shanmei** 山莓 *shan-may*
raspberry

**shanyangrou** 山羊肉
*shan-yang-ro*
mutton

**shao** 少 *shao* little

**shaobing** 烧饼 *shao-bing*
fried sweet with sesame,
see Dim sum, p. 40

**shaojiu** 烧酒 *shao-jioh*
spirit

**shaoliang** 少量 *shao-
liang* morsel

**shaomai** 烧卖 *shao-mai*,
see Dim sum, p. 40

**shaoshang** 烧伤 *shao-
shang* burned

**shaoxingjiu** 绍兴酒 *shao-
sing-jioh*, see Beverages, p. 23

**shaozi** 勺子 *shao-ds*
tablespoon

**she** 蛇 *sh* snake

**shen** 肾 *shen* kidney

**shen** 深 *shen* dark

**sheng** 升 *sheng* liter

**shengchou wang** 升抽王
*sheng-cho wang* light soy
sauce, see Condiments
and main ingredients,
p. 31

**shengde** 生的 *sheng-d*
raw

**shengjiang** 生姜 *sheng-
jiang* ginger, see
Condiments and main
ingredients, p. 33

**shenme shihou** 什么时候
*shen-m shr-ho* when

**shenzang** 肾脏 *shen-dsan*
kidney

**shi** 试 *shr* to try

**shikebiao** 时刻表 *shr-ke-
biao* timetable

**shiliu** 石榴 *shr-liu*
pomegranate

**shipin** 食品 *shr-pin* food

**shipin shangdian** 食品商
店 *shr-pin shang-dien*
grocery store

**shitang** 食堂 *shr-tang* canteen

**shiwu** 食物 *shr-woo* diet

**shiwu zhongdu** 食物中毒 *shr-woo joong-doo* food poisoning

**shizi** 柿子 *shr-ds* persimmon

**shizi tou** 獅子头 *shr-ds toe*, see Regional dishes, p. 67

**shou** 瘦 *sho* lean

**shoukuanchu** 收款处 *sho-kwan-choo* checkout

**shoukuanyuan** 收款员 *sho-kwan-ywen* cashier

**shoutibao** 手提包 *sho-tee-bao* handbag

**shouyinji** 收音机 *sho-yin-jee* radio

**shu** 熟 *shoo* ripe

**shuan** 涮 *shwan*, see Gastronomic terms, p. 98

**shuanggou daqu** 双沟大曲 *shwang-go da-choo*, see Beverages, p. 22

**shuanyangrou** 涮羊肉 *shwan-yang-ro* Mongolian fondu, see Regional dishes, p. 61

**shuazi** 刷子 *shwa-ds* brush

**shucai** 蔬菜 *shoo-tsai* vegetable

**shucai chaofan** 蔬菜炒饭 *shoo-tsai chao-fan* stir-fried rice with vegetables, see National dishes, p. 55

**shucai chaomian** 蔬菜炒面 *shoo-tsai chao-mien* stir-fried noodles with vegetables, see National dishes, p. 55

**shucaiguan** 蔬菜馆 *shoo-tsai-gwan* vegetarian restaurant

**shui** 水 *shweh* water

**shuiguo** 水果 *shweh-gwo* fruit

**shuiguo shala** 水果沙拉 *shweh-gwo sha-la* fruit salad

**shuihu** 水壶 *shweh-hoo* carafe

**shuijiao** 水饺 *shweh-jiao* boiled ravioli

**shuijing xiaren** 水晶虾仁 *shweh-jing sia-ren* crystal prawns, see Regional dishes, p. 62 and Recipes, p. 89

**shuisheng youqiao dongwu** 水生有壳动物

*shweh-sheng yo-chiao dong-woo* crustaceans

**shufu** 舒服 *shoo-foo* comfortable

**shuweicao** 鼠尾草 *shoo-way-tsao* sage

**si** 丝 *s* thin strip, see Gastronomic terms, p. 98

**Sichuan lazi ji** 四川辣子鸡 *s-chwan la-ds jee*, see Regional dishes, p. 71

**Sichuan qiezi** 四川茄子 *s-chwan chie-ds* Sichuan-style eggplant, see Regional dishes, p. 71 and Recipes, p. 90

**shijin** 什锦 *shr-jin* mixed

**songruan** 松软 *soong-rwan* soft

**su** 酥 *soo* crisp

**su shijin** 素什锦 *soo shr-jin* mixed vegetables with tofu, see Regional dishes, p. 71 and Recipes, p. 91

**suan** 酸 *swan* sour

**suanla** 酸辣 *swan-la* spicy and sour, see Gastronomic terms, p. 98

**suanla luobo** 酸辣萝卜

*swan-la lwo-boh*, see National dishes, p. 55

**suanla tang** 酸辣汤 *swan-la tang* spicy and sour soup, see National dishes, p. 56 and Recipes, p. 92

**suanniunai** 酸牛奶 *swan-niu-nai* yogurt

**suantian tudousi** 酸甜土豆丝 *swan-tien too-doe-s*, see National dishes, p. 56

**suantou ya** 蒜头鸭 *swan-toe ya*, see Regional dishes, p. 62

**suchao douya** 素炒豆芽 *soo-chao doe-ya*, see National dishes, p. 56

**sun** 笋 *soon* bamboo shoots, see Condiments and main ingredients, p. 28

**suoyou** 所有 *swo-yo* all, everything

**taiduo** 太多 *dai-dwo* too much

**taitai** 太太 *tai-tai* lady

**tang** 糖 *tang* caramel; sugar

**tang** 汤 *tang* soup, see

Gastronomic terms,
p. 98

**tang yuan** 汤圆 *tang ywen,*
see Regional dishes, p. 72

**tangchi** 汤匙 *tang-chr*
tablespoon

**tangcu** 糖醋 *tang-tsoo* bitter-
sweet, sweet and sour, see
Gastronomic terms, p. 98

**tangcu daxia** 糖醋大虾
*tang-tsoo da-sia,* see
National dishes, p. 56

**tangcu yu** 糖醋渔 *tang-
tsoo yoo* sweet and sour fish,
see National dishes, p. 56

**tangde** 汤的 *tang-d* boiling

**tangdai** 唐代 *tang-dai*
sweetner

**tangguang** 糖罐 *tang-
gwang* sugar basin

**tangniaobing** 糖尿病
*tang-niao-bing* diabetes

**tangniaobing huanzhe**
糖尿病患者 *tang-niao-
bing hwan-j* diabetic

**tangshui** 糖水 *tang-shweh*
syrup

**tangwan** 汤碗 *tang-wan*
soup tureen

**tao** 桃 *tao* peach

**taocan** 套餐 *tao-tsan* set
menu

**techan** 特产 *te-chan*
specialty

**ti** 梯 *tee* stairs

**tian** 甜 *tien* sweet (adj.)

**tiancai** 甜菜 *tien-tsai*
beet

**tiandian** 甜点 *tien-dien*
confectionery

**tianjiaji** 添加剂 *tien-jia-
jee* additive

**tianjiu** 甜酒 *tien-jioh* rum

**tianmian jiang** 甜面酱
*tien-mien jiang* sweet
soya paste, see
Condiments and main
ingredients, p. 29

**tiansuan jiang** 甜酸酱
*tien-swan jiang* sweet and
sour sauce, see
Condiments and main
ingredients, p. 30

**tiaoweiliao** 调味料 *tiao-
way-liao* condiment

**tibao** 提包 *tee-bao* bag

**tingchezhan** 停车站
*ting-che-jan* car park

**tongyide** 同一的 *tong-ee-
d* equal

**tousu** 投诉 *toe-soo* complaint

**tuan** 团 *twan* group

**tudou** 土豆 *too-doe* potato

**tui** 退 *tweh* leg

**tuihui** 退回 *tweh-hweh* reimbursement

**tuopan** 托盘 *twoh-pan* tray

**tuzi** 兔子 *too-ds* rabbit, hare

**waiguoren** 外国人 *wai-gwo-ren* foreigner

**waihui** 外汇 *wai-hweh* currency

**wan** 碗 *wan* bowl, cup

**wan** 晚 *wan* delay

**wangchao** 王朝 *wang-chao*, see Beverages, p. 24

**wandou** 豌豆 *wan-doe* pea

**wandouzhou** 豌豆粥 *wan-doe-jo*, see Dim sum, p. 40

**wanfan** 晚饭 *wan-fan* dinner

**wanshang** 晚上 *wan-shang* evening

**wanzi** 丸子 *wan-ds* meatball

**wei** 味 *way* taste; flavor; smell

**weiba** 尾巴 *way-ba* tail

**weidao** 味道 *way-dao* taste, flavor

**weidaohao** 味道好 *way-dao-hao* flavorsome

**wenjian** 文件 *wen-jien* document

**weijing** 味精 *way-jing* monosodium glutamate

**weikou** 胃口 *way-ko* appetite

**weimeisi** 味美思 *way-may-s* vermouth

**wendu** 温度 *wen-doo* temperature

**weishengshu** 维生素 *way-sheng-shoo* vitamin

**weishengzhi** 卫生纸 *way-sheng-jr* toilet paper

**weishiji** 威士忌 *way-shr-jee* whisky

**weishu** 未熟 *way-shoo* bitter, sour

**weizhong** 味重 *way-joong* strong (flavor)

**wenzi** 蚊子 *wen-ds* mosquito

**woju** 莴苣 *woh-joo* lettuce

**woniu** 蜗牛 *woh-niu* snail

**wucai chaofan** 五彩炒饭

*woo-tsai chao-fan*, see Regional dishes, p. 65

**wufan** 午饭 *woo-fan* lunch

**wugui** 乌龟 *woo-gweh* turtle

**wuhuaguo** 无花果 *woo-hwa-gwo* fig

**wuliangye** 五粮液 *woo-liang-yeh*, see Beverages, p. 22

**wulongcha** 乌龙茶 *woo-long-cha* Oolong tea, see Beverages, p. 16

**wunei** 屋内 *woo-nay* under cover

**wuxiang fen** 五香粉 *woo-siang fen* five-spice powder, see Condiments and main ingredients, p. 29

**wuxiang paigu** 五香排骨 *woo-siang pai-goo* pork chops with five spices, see Regional dishes, p. 68 and Recipes, p. 94

**wuxiang xunyu** 五香熏鱼 *woo-siang soon-yoo*, see National dishes, p. 56

**xi** 洗 *see* to wash

**xi** 细 *see* thin

**xia** 虾 *sia* shrimp

**xiabian** 下边 *sia-bien* under

**xian** 线 *sien* thread

**xian** 馅 *sien* filling, stuffing

**xian heye fan** 馅荷叶饭 *sien heh-yeh fan*, see Regional dishes, p. 65

**xian mogu** 鲜蘑菇 *sien moh-goo* fresh mushrooms

**xian shuiguo** 鲜水果 *sien shweh-gwo* fresh fruit

**xianbing** 馅饼 *sien-bing*, see Dim sum, p. 40

**xiangbingjiu** 香槟酒 *siang-bing-jioh* champagne

**xiangcai** 香菜 *siang-tsai* coriander; parsley

**xiangchang** 香肠 *siang-chang* sausage

**xiangdao** 向导 *siang-dao* guide (person)

**Xianggang** 香港 *siang-gang* Hong Kong

**xianggu** 香菇 *siang-goo* truffle

**xiangjiao** 香蕉 *siang-jiao* banana

**xiangsuji** 香酥鸡 *siang-soo-jee*, see National dishes, p. 56

**xiangsu ya 香酥鸭** *siang-soo ya*, see Regional dishes, p. 72

**xiangyan 香烟** *siang-yen* cigarette

**xiangzi 箱子** *siang-ds* luggage, suitcase

**xianqian 现钱** *sien-chien* cash

**xiansheng 先生** *sien-sheng* gentleman

**xianrou 咸肉** *sien-ro* bacon

**xianzai 现在** *sien-dsai* now

**xiao 小** *siao* small

**xiaobiandou 小扁豆** *siao-bien-doe* lentils

**xiaochidian 小吃店** *siao-chr-dien* cheap, informal restaurant

**xiaofei 小费** *siao-fay* tip

**xiaohua 消化** *siao-hwa* digestion

**xiaohua bushi 消化不食** *siao-hwa boo-shr* indigestion

**xiaohuanggua 小黄瓜** *siao-hwang-gwa* gherkin

**xiaojie 小姐** *siao-jie* young lady

**xiaokuai 小块** *siao-kwai* morsel

**xiaomi 小米** *siao-mee* millet

**xiaoniu 小牛** *siao-niu* veal

**xiaoshanyang 小山羊** *siao-shan-yang* kid (baby goat)

**xiaoshao 小勺** *siao-shao* teaspoon

**xiaoshi 小时** *siao-shr* hour, time

**xiaoshou 销售** *siao-shoe* market

**xiaren guoba 虾仁锅巴** *sia-ren gwo-ba*, see Regional dishes, p. 68

**xiaren tang 虾仁汤** *sia-ren tang*, see National dishes, p. 57

**xicai 西菜** *see-tsai* Western food

**xie 写** *sie* to write

**xierou jiao 蟹肉饺** *sie-ro jiao*, see Dim sum, p. 40

**xiexie 谢谢** *sie-sie* thank you

**xigua 西瓜** *see-gwa* watermelon, melon

**xihongshi 西红柿** *see-hong-shr* tomato

**xihongshi chao dan 西红柿炒蛋** *see-hong-shr*

**chao dan**, see National dishes, p. 57

**xihuan** 喜欢 *see-hwan* to like, to want

**xinfeng** 信封 *sin-feng* envelope

**xing** 行 *sing* to work (function)

**xing** 姓 *sing* surname

**xing** 杏 *sing* apricot

**xingli** 行李 *sing-lee* luggage

**xingqi** 星期 *sing-chee* week

**xingren** 杏仁 *sing-ren* almond

**xingren doufu** 杏仁豆腐 *sing-ren toefoo*, see Regional dishes, p. 62

**xining jipian** 西柠鸡片 *see-nin jee-pien* chicken with lemon, see Regional dishes, p. 65

**xinxian** 新鲜 *sing-sien* fresh

**xinyongka** 信用卡 *sing-yong-ca* credit card

**xinyuexing mianbao** 新月形面包 *sing-yweh-sing mien-bao* croissant, brioche

**xishi zaofan** 西式早饭 *see-shr dsao-fan* Western-style breakfast

**xishoujian** 洗手间 *see-sho-jien* toilet

**xiyan** 吸烟 *see-yen* to smoke

**xuepi** 削皮 *sweh-pee* to peel

**xueqie** 雪茄 *sweh-chie* cigar

**xueyu** 鳕渔 *sweh-yoo* cod

**xun** 熏 *soon* smoked

**xunguiyu** 熏鲑渔 *soon-gweh-yoo* smoked salmon

**xusuizi** 续随子 *soo-sweh-ds* capers

**xuyao** 需要 *soo-yao* to need

**ya** 鸭 *ya* duck

**yajia tang** 鸭架汤 *ya-jia tang*, see Regional dishes, p. 62

**yanba** 盐巴 *yen-ba* salt

**yande** 腌的 *yen-d* salty

**yang** 羊 *yang* lamb

**yangang** 盐缸 *yen-gang* salt cellar

**yanghe daqu** 羊河大曲 *yang-heh da-choo*, see Beverages, p. 22

**yangji** 洋蓟 *yang-jee* artichoke

**yangtai** 阳台 *yang-tai*
terrace

**Yangzhou chaofan** 扬州
炒饭 *yang-joo chao-fan*
Yangzhou-style fried rice,
see Regional dishes,
p. 68

**yanhui** 宴会 *yen-hweh*
banquet

**yanhuigang** 烟灰缸 *yen-hweh-gang* ash tray

**yanji** 阉鸡 *yen-jee* capon

**yanmai** 燕麦 *yen-mai*
oats

**yanpao** 腌泡 *yen-pao*
marinated

**yanse** 颜色 *yen-s* color

**yansui** 芫荽 *yen-sweh*
coriander (spice)

**yao** 要 *yao* to want, desire

**yaodian** 药店 *yao-dien*
pharmacy

**yaofang** 药方 *yao-fang*
medical prescription

**yaoguo** 腰果 *yao-gwo*
cashew nuts

**yaoqian** 要钱 *yao-chien*
to debit

**yaqian** 牙签 *ya-chien*
toothpicks

**yaorou** 腰肉 *yao-ro*
loin

**ye** 也 *yeh* also, too

**yeguangbei** 夜光杯 *yeh-gwang-bay*, see
Beverages, p. 24

**yeti** 液体 *yeh-tee* liquid

**yewei** 野味 *yeh-way*
game

**yezi** 椰子 *yeh-ds* coconut

**Yidali** 意大利 *ee-da-lee* Italy

**yidaliren** 意大利人 *ee-da-lee-ren* Italian (native of Italy)

**yidaliyu** 意大利语 *ee-da-lee-yoo* Italian (language of Italy)

**yimaojian** 衣帽间 *ee-mao-jien* cloakroom

**yin** 阴 *yin* moon

**yingbi** 硬币 *ying-bee*
coinage

**Yingguo** 英国 *ying-gwo*
Great Britain

**yingguoren** 英国人 *ying-gwo-ren* native of England

**yingyu** 英语 *ying-yoo*
English (language)

**yingtao** 樱桃 *ying-tao* cherry

**yingzuidou** 鹰嘴豆 *ying-dsweh-doe* chick-peas

**yinhang** 银行 *ying-hang*

bank

**yinliao** 饮料 *yin-liao* beverage

**yiyangde** 一样的 *ee-yang-d* equal

**yizi** 椅子 *ee-ds* chair

**you** 有 *yo* to have, to be

**you** 油 *yo* oil, sauce

**youbao ji** 油爆鸡 *yo-bao jee*, see Regional dishes, p. 62

**youbing** 油饼 *yo-bing*, see Dim sum, p. 41

**youde** 有的 *yo-d* some

**youlan** 游览 *yo-lan* trip, excursion

**youli** 油梨 *yo-lee* avocado

**youni** 油泥 *yo-nee* greasy

**youpiao** 邮票 *yo-piao* postage stamp

**youtiao** 油条 *yo-tiao*, see Dim sum, p. 41

**youyingyang** 有营养 *yo-ying-yang* nutritious

**youyongchi** 游泳池 *yo-yong-chr* swimming pool

**youyu** 鱿鱼 *yo-yoo* squid

**youyu guoba** 鱿鱼锅巴 *yo-yoo gwo-ba*, see

Regional dishes, p. 72

**youzi** 柚子 *yo-ds* grapefruit

**yu** 渔 *yoo* fish

**yuan** 元 *ywen* to gather

**yuanliao** 原料 *ywen-liao* ingredient

**yuantang** 原汤 *ywen-tang* broth

**yuanxiao** 元宵 *ywen-siao*, see Dim sum, p. 41

**yudingde** 预定的 *yoo-ding-d* reserved

**yuebing** 月饼 *yweh-bing* moon biscuits, see Dim sum, p. 41

**yuegui** 月桂 *yweh-gweh* laurel

**yuehui** 约会 *yweh-hweh* appointment

**yueju** 越橘 *yweh-joo* blueberry

**yufu** 预付 *yoo-foo* deposit (part payment)

**yumi** 玉米 *yoo-mee* maize

**yumi bangzi** 玉米棒子 *yoo-mee bang-ds* ear (cereal)

**yumifen** 玉米粉 *yoo-mee-fen* cornstarch, see Condiments and main ingredients, p. 26

**yumipian** 玉米片 *yoo-mee-pien* cornflakes

**yumi tang** 玉米汤 *yoo-mee tang* corn soup, see National dishes, p. 57

**yunshu** 运输 *yoon-shoo* transport

**yurou** 渔肉 *yoo-ro* fish

**yuwei** 余味 *yoo-way* aftertaste

**yuxiang rousi** 渔香肉丝 *yoo-siang ro-s*, see Regional dishes, p. 72

**yuxiang you** 渔香油 *yoo-siang yo* fish-flavored sauce, see Condiments and main ingredients, p. 30

**yuxiang zhugan** 渔香猪干 *yoo-siang joo-gan*, see Regional dishes, p. 72

**zai** 再 *dsai* again (adv.)

**zai zher** 在这儿 *dsai jer* here

**zanba** 糌粑 *dsam-pa*, see Beverages, p. 17

**zang** 脏 *dsang* dirty

**zangqi** 脏器 *dsang-chee* entrails

**zaofan** 早饭 *dsao-fan* breakfast

**zaozi** 枣子 *dsao-ds* date, see Condiments and main ingredients, p. 27

**zha** 炸 *ja* fried, see Cooking methods, p. 48 Gastronomic terms, p. 98

**zha tudoutiao** 炸土豆条 *ja too-doe-tiao* fried potatoes

**zhagao** 炸糕 *ja-gao*, see Dim sum, p. 42

**zhan** 站 *jan* (bus) stop

**zhangcha kaoya** 樟茶烤鸭 *jang-cha kao-ya* smoked duck with tea and camphor, see Regional dishes, p. 73

**zhangdan** 帐单 *jang-dan* bill

**zhaodeqian** 找的钱 *jao-d-chien* change

**zhayuanbing** 炸圆饼 *ja ywen-bing* fried donut

**zhege** 这个 *je-g* this

**zheng** 蒸 *jeng* steaming

**zhengming** 证明 *jeng-ming* document

zhengqi 蒸汽 *jeng-chee*
steam

zheng 蒸 *jeng*, see
Gastronomic terms, p. 98

zhengzhu rouwan 蒸猪
肉丸 *jeng-joo ro-wan*,
see National dishes, p. 57

zhentou 枕头 *jen-toe*
pillow

zhenzi 榛子 *jen-ds*
hazelnut

zhi 汁 *jr* juice

zhi 纸 *jr* paper

zhi 支 *jr* to pay

zhifu 支付 *jr-foo* payment

zhima 芝麻 *jr-ma*
sesame, see Condiments
and main ingredients,
p. 32

zhima you 芝麻油 *jr-ma
yo* sesame oil, see
Condiments and main
ingredients, p. 29

zhinan 指南 *jr-nan* guide (book)

zhipiao 支票 *jr-piao*
check

zhishao 至少 *jr-shao* at
least

zhishi 指示 *jr-shr* to show

zhong 重 *joong* heavy

zhongdianzhan 终点站
*joong-dien-jan* terminus

Zhongguo 中国 *joong-
gwo* China

zhongguoren 中国人
*joong-gwo-ren* native of
China

Zhongguo renmin
gongheguo 中国人民
共和国 *joong-gwo ren-
min goong-heh-gwo*
People's Republic of China

zhongzai 中菜 *joong-
dsai* Chinese cuisine

zhou 粥 *jo*, see
Gastronomic terms, p. 99

zhu 煮 *joo* to boil, to
cook, see Gastronomic
terms, p. 99

zhu jidan 煮鸡蛋 *joo
jee-dan* hard-boiled egg

zhuachao haixian 抓炒
海鲜 *jwa-chao hai-sien*,
see Recipes, p. 95

zhuancha 砖茶 *jwan-cha*
brick tea, see Beverages,
p. 16

zhuanpan 转盘 *jwan-pan*
rotating serving platform

zhuazi 爪子 *jwa-ds* leg

**zhude** 煮的 *joo-d*
boiled

**zhunbeihao** 准备好 *joon-bay-hao* ready (adj.)

**zhuobu** 桌布 *jwo-boo*
tablecloth

**zhuozi** 桌子 *jwo-ds* table

**zhurou** 猪肉 *joo-ro*
pork

**zhusi chaofan** 猪丝炒饭
*joo-s chao-fan*, see
National dishes, p. 57

**zhusi chaomian** 猪丝炒面
*joo-s chao-mien*, see
National dishes, p. 57

**zhusun** 竹笋 *joo-soon*
bamboo shoots, see
Condiments and main
ingredients, p. 28

**zhuxiaohua** 助消化 *joo-siao-hwa* digestive

**zhuyeqing** 竹叶青 *joo-yeh-ching*, see Beverages, p. 22

**zhuzi** 竹子 *joo-ds* bamboo

**ziyou shichang** 自由市场
*ds-yo shr-chang* market

**ziyu** 鲻渔 *ds-yoo* mullet

**zizhucan** 自主餐 *ds-joo-tsan* buffet

**zizhushi** 自主式 *ds-joo-shr* self-service

**zongzi** 粽子 *dsoong-ds*,
see Dim sum, p. 42

**zoulu** 走路 *dso-loo*
to walk, to go
on foot

**zu** 组 *dsoo* group

**zugou** 足够 *dsoo-go*
enough

**zui ji** 醉鸡 *dsweh jee*
drunken chicken, see
Regional dishes, p. 62

**zunyu** 鳟渔 *dsoon-yoo* trout

**zuoliao** 作料 *dswo-liao*
condiment; ingredient;
spice

# INDEX

NOTE ON PRONUNCIATION
• 3

INTRODUCTION • 4
What the Chinese eat • 5

WHERE TO EAT • 7
The Chinese table • 8
The banquet • 9

BEVERAGES • 12
Tea • 13
Making tea according to the
rules • 17
Dishes with tea • 18
Wine and liqueurs • 19
Liqueurs • 20
Rice wines • 23
Grape wines • 24
Beer • 25

CONDIMENTS AND MAIN
INGREDIENTS • 26

CUISINE AND MEDICINE • 35

DIM SUM • 37

CHINESE CUISINE IN THE
WEST • 43

COOKING METHODS • 47

NATIONAL DISHES • 50

REGIONAL DISHES • 58
Beijing • 58
Canton • 63
Shanghai • 66
Sichuan • 68

RECIPES • 74

GASTRONOMIC TERMS • 96

CONVERSATION • 100

DATE AND CALENDAR • 103

EATING OUT •
Reservations • 105
Information • 106
Ordering • 107

ENTERTAINMENT • 111

GOURMET SHOPPING • 113

GREETINGS • 115

HOLIDAYS • 116

HOTELS •
Reservations • 119
Reception • 120
Room Service • 121

INFORMATION • 122

MONEY • 124

NUMBERS • 128

PAYING • 130

PRONUNCIATION • 131

SIGNALS • 132

TAXI • 134

TEA • 135

TELEPHONE • 136

TIME • 138

TIPS • 139

TOILETTE • 140

UNITS OF MEASURE • 141

GASTRONOMIC
DICTIONARY • 143